Betty Rae White

Your Children's Faith

Your Children's Faith

A
GUIDE
FOR PARENTS

by

Florence M. Taylor

1964

DOUBLEDAY & COMPANY, INC.

GARDEN CITY, NEW YORK

LIBRARY OF CONGRESS CATALOG CARD NUMBER 64–19273
COPYRIGHT © 1964 BY FLORENCE M. TAYLOR
ALL RIGHTS RESERVED
PRINTED IN THE UNITED STATES OF AMERICA
FIRST EDITION

FOREWORD

During the last quarter of a century a growing trend has appeared in writings in the field of Christian education. It began with a few single voices here and there and gathered volume over the years. Now with a unanimous voice Christian educators declare, "The development of the Christian faith in children and their Christian education is primarily the task of the parents. The Church can help but it cannot do the job alone. The home must reassume its responsibility in this area."

Faced with this reiterated challenge, many parents are becoming aware of their need for deeper knowledge of the bases of their Christian faith, for clearer insights into the guiding purposes of their family life, for greater skill in achieving more Christian relationships within and beyond the family group. And along with a recognition of these needs has gone an admission that for many of these parents the Bible is practically a closed book.

This book is an attempt to meet some of these needs. It is the author's conviction that numbers of parents, having been challenged to accept responsibility for the Christian education of their children, are accepting that challenge. They are earnestly seeking for a deeper understanding of their Christian heritage. They are taking back into their own hands tasks that had been allowed to slip through their fingers.

Some of these parents are gathering together in small discussion groups to think together about the faith of their children. Some are discovering in Bible study groups the relevance of the Bible for these modern days, and are finding in its pages sustenance and strength for the spiritual life. Some are establishing a "family altar" in their homes. Many are consciously striving for more Christian relationships in the family circle and beyond. Some are deepening the family ties to the Church, and are finding encouragement and support in the larger fellowship.

Once again Christian parents are beginning to take seriously the ancient commands:

> What does the Lord your God require of you, but to fear the Lord your God, to walk in all his ways, to love him, to serve the Lord your God with all your heart and with all your soul, and to keep the commandments and statutes of the Lord . . . ? You shall therefore lay up these words of mine in your heart and in your soul; . . . And you shall teach them to your children, talking of them when you are sitting in your house, and when you are walking by the way, and when you lie down, and when you rise. (Deuteronomy 10:12–13; 11:18–19)

The present book seeks to help parents in two specific areas. Part I, "The Christian Home," deals with the Christian family as a potential redemptive society, "the Church within thy house." Such a family tries to provide for each member a warm, human love that reflects, however feebly, the divine love of God. It tries to sustain and nourish the best in each individual, as each strives to attain his optimal development. It participates in the life and ministry of the Christian Church of which it is a part.

Because an understanding knowledge of the Bible is so basically important to all Christian living, Part II, "The Bible and Your Child," challenges parents to clarify their own religious beliefs and tries to give them a frame of reference that will help them in using the Bible intelligently with their children. It attempts to open up for them some of the spiritual resources available in the Bible so that the family may discover "the unsearchable riches of Christ" for joyous and triumphant living.

CONTENTS

PART I

The Christian Home

The world needed a saving faith and the formula was that such a faith comes by a particular kind of fellowship. Jesus was deeply concerned for the continuation of his redemptive work after the close of his earthly existence, and his chosen method was *the formation of a redemptive society.* He did not form an army, establish a headquarters or even write a book. All he did was to collect a few unpromising men, inspire them with a sense of his vocation and theirs and build their lives into an intensive fellowship of affection, worship and work.

ELTON TRUEBLOOD,
Alternative to Futility
(New York: Harper & Brothers, 1948), p. 29.

CHAPTER 1

The Strength of the Family

Elton Trueblood has pointed out in *Alternative to Futility* that the redemptive fellowship of Jesus and his disciples was not an accident of history. On the contrary, it seems to have been the deliberately chosen method whereby Jesus planned for the continuation of his unfinished task—the lifting of all mankind to a new relationship with God and with each other.

Dr. Trueblood goes on to point out that this first fellowship was made up of quite ordinary people and that several of them displayed quite extraordinary weaknesses and failings. Judas was there, who, for reasons no one has ever understood (least of all perhaps Judas himself), betrayed the Master whom he loved. Peter was there, weak and cowardly even at a late point in his association with Jesus. But Jesus discerned within the vacillating, uncertain character of Peter, the potential "rock" of moral integrity. James and John were there, wanting assurance of prestige and powers in the kingdom they expected Jesus to establish. Others were there in that little fellowship, so inconspicuous in their ordinariness that all we know of them is a list of names—and even the lists given in the Scripture do not agree.[1]

Quite ordinary people! And yet that little group of weak and faulty human beings *was* a redemptive society. In one of the miracles of history they justified Jesus' faith in them. They

[1] See Matthew 10:2–4 and Acts 1:12–13.

generated a spiritual force unmatched, before or since, and so against seemingly insurmountable odds ensured the survival and continuation of the Christian faith.

Since its beginning the Christian Church at its best has been a redemptive fellowship, a fellowship not of saints but of confessed sinners, including in its membership people holding vastly different points of view but united in a common loyalty to God as revealed in Jesus.

Look at the Christian Church as critically as you please. Admit all its sins of omission and commission. It still has an amazing record of individuals whose lives, under its influence, have achieved heroic dimensions, who have been strengthened to accomplish miracles of service to suffering humanity, and who have met frustration, failure, and martyrdom with unshakable faith in God. For almost two thousand years the Christian Church has been the creator and sustainer of a winged faith for thousands of people.

"The world needed a saving faith, and the formula was that such a faith comes by a particular kind of fellowship." Today our families need a saving faith, and the formula is still the same: "Such a faith comes by a particular kind of fellowship."

For parents this is a startling and quickening thought. It is easy to assume that faith comes in various ways—perhaps by accepting certain tenets of belief, by suppressing all doubts and questions, by submitting to certain disciplines, or by performing prescribed routine acts of religious observance.

That the Christian faith comes by "a particular kind of fellowship" opens up new directions for creative thinking, new possibilities for creative action in family living.

It is the contention of this book that one mark that distinguishes the Christian home from other homes in our modern American society is its relatedness to the redemptive fellowship of the Christian Church.

Let us hasten to avoid misunderstanding, however, by admitting that by no means all Church-related homes are "redemptive fellowships." Obviously, there are degrees, both quantitative and qualitative of Church-relatedness. It remains true that neither an individual nor a family can live a Christian life in isolation. The very essence of Christianity is in human relationships.

The search for God has followed many paths. Families in other faiths have found high values and have lived noble lives, but Christianity began and has continued through the years as a redemptive fellowship, and a Christian family by definition is a part of the wider group.

In the exciting days when new little Christian churches were springing up along the routes of Paul's dangerous journeys, he wrote: "To Philemon . . . and the church in your house: Grace to you. . . ." (Philemon 1:3) And again: "Aquila and Prisca, together with the church in their house, send you hearty greetings. . . ." (1 Corinthians 16:19)

"The church in thy house" as it occurs in Paul's letter, refers of course to the little group of Christians who met together in some home to worship and plan together, and to share in the sacrament of the Lord's Supper, long before there were any church buildings.

> Nowhere in the New Testament does the word Church mean a building . . . The Church is always a company of worshipping people who have given their hearts and pledged their lives to Jesus Christ.[2]

The Church today is still people. The Church is the Church not just on Sunday morning when its members gather to worship. It is still the Church on Monday and on Tuesday and all through the week as its members carry on their daily lives in their homes and communities.

For us today the phrase "the church in thy house" may come to have a more intimate meaning as we apply it to our family. The Church is in thy house. "Grace to you."

The family in search of a winged faith, consciously trying to transform itself into a redemptive fellowship, will recognize itself as a part of the greater fellowship, the Christian

[2] William Barclay in *The Mind of St. Paul* (New York: Harper & Brothers, 1958), pp. 237–38.

Church, will participate in its corporate worship, and share in its ministry to this fear-ridden, hate-filled world.

Fortunate indeed are those individuals who experience the redemptive fellowship in two powerful agencies—the Christian home and the Christian Church.

CHAPTER 2

The Loving Fellowship

Many attempts have been made to define the Church, of which each Christian family is a part, and to describe its function, which the Christian family also shares. The genius of Paul caught its essence in a mere four words: "the body of Christ."[1]

To be "the body of Christ" is a daring challenge. Even to think of this term applied to our individual lives is to be confronted with a sense of utter and complete failure. It seems like sacrilege. Jesus in his brief ministry set in motion forces that are changing the world. Even the most dedicated Christian, contrasting his life with that of Jesus, must shrink from the resulting revelation, and must surely hear God's judgmental voice in his heart:

> Look at the Man . . . and look at yourself!
> Sons of the same Father, but who would dream it?
> The firefly and the sun are no more unlike than you two.[2]

[1] See William Barclay's interpretation of this phrase in *The Mind of St. Paul*, pp. 241–51.
[2] Hermann Hagedorn, *The Bomb that Fell on America* (California: Pacific Coast Publishing Co., 1947), p. 43. Used by permission of Hermann Hagedorn.

Each of us needs the faith that can also hear God's re-assurance:

> The firefly can't do anything about it. You can.
> That's a part of the miracle of the soul . . .
>   that the human creature can change, become
>   different, grow out of the nature of the firefly,
>   grow into the quality of the sun.
> The worm and the moth, the cocoon and the butterfly,
>   you—and what God wants you to be.[3]

"You are the body of Christ," wrote Paul. How did he dare make this claim for the little group of first-century Christians to whom he wrote? Were they perhaps very different from us, much better people than we are? It seems unlikely. Paul had many occasions to upbraid them. Listen to these verses from an earlier chapter of the same letter:

> Do you not know that the unrighteous will not inherit the king-dom of God? Do not be deceived; neither the immoral, nor idola-ters, nor adulterers, nor homosexuals, nor thieves, nor the greedy, nor drunkards, nor revilers, nor robbers, will inherit the kingdom of God. And such were some of you. (1 Corinthians 6:9–11)

Quite ordinary people, apparently, even as were the twelve disciples. And yet Paul dared to call them "the body of Christ." Can there be some deeper meaning here not evident at first glance? No one individual member of the fellowship would dare apply to himself these words "the body of Christ"; and surely the Church is made up of its individual members and has no separate existence apart from them. But is it perhaps true, that what would be sacrilege for any one of us alone, may in some strangely mysterious way be true of all of us together in the redemptive fellowship?

Each of us is capable at times of small bits of Christlike living. Each of us once in a while puts into practice the principles of living to which we give lip service. Each of us in rare moments lives by the law of love sufficiently to catch a glimpse of what true Christlike living might be.

What if, in the marvelous economy of God, these rare

[3] *Ibid.*

bits of fumbling, "firefly" efforts can be gathered up and treasured, and made to produce results far beyond our expectations or desserts? Once in a while we catch a glimpse of the mysterious way in which God magnifies the efforts of individuals.

Because some of us give a casual dollar to Church World Service, thousands of starving babies in distant lands are fed.

Because a few people become aware of lonely students from foreign lands living in their vicinity, and make an effort to show friendliness, countless strong ties of friendship now reach across separating oceans into other lands.

Because a thirteen-year-old American Negro boy living in Italy reads about Albert Schweitzer and is moved with a great desire to send medical supplies to the doctor's African hospital, a chain of events is started which results in a gift to Dr. Schweitzer of medicines worth $400,000.[4]

Truly in these events we can see the body of Christ ministering to the needs of the world.

The paragraphs above have pointed out the importance of individual ministry, the amazing way in which one person may be used of God to further his eternal purposes.

In a larger and deeper way the Church itself has fulfilled its function as "the body of Christ" at work in the world. Fumblingly and imperfectly (like its individual members) it has struggled on, guilty often of denying the Christ it worships, sinning frequently against its own law of love, committing heinous crimes in the very name of religion, but somehow never completely losing its high vision of service. Repenting, and receiving forgiveness, reforming only to sin again, it has somehow out of its travail brought forth new understandings, new visions, new dedication.

If the Church exists to be the body of Christ still carrying on his ministry in the world, and if the Christian family shares in this responsibility, it may be helpful briefly to consider the

4 See "To Dr. Schweitzer with Love" by Morton Tuner in *Coronet*, April 1960.

various ways in which Jesus himself carried on his God-given task.

Jesus' ministry consisted in the total giving of himself to meet the needs of every person with whom he came in contact. Steadily, consistently, he gave himself, his strength, his courage, his faith, his love, to every least person, no matter how seemingly unimportant or unworthy. His giving of himself reached its climax in his death on the cross, where he suffered the worst that evil could do, in order to meet the needs of all mankind.

It is given to comparatively few of his faithful followers through the ages to share in his ministry of suffering and martyrdom. The lesser ministry of loving self-forgetting service, of patient day-by-day doing of deeds of Christian love has been carried on by uncounted thousands in every generation.

THE FOUR ASPECTS OF JESUS' MINISTRY

A study of Jesus' day-by-day life reveals four ways through which he ministered to those around him, ways through which his Church in every generation has sought to continue his ministry.

Jesus came "preaching the good news," making *a joyous proclamation*. He proclaimed the good news of God's true nature, of his love for each person, and therefore of the importance of each individual. He proclaimed God's claim to the wholehearted, single-minded devotion of his people, and God's unfailing and always available strength for triumphant living in spite of all life's tragedies. He proclaimed God's forgiving and redeeming love even for sinful people.

Jesus ministered to the needs of men *by teaching*—teaching by radiant, lucid words, by graphic, unforgettable stories; teaching even more by powerful living, by deeds consistent with and inseparable from his spoken words.

Jesus performed *a ministry of service,* a ministry invariably and instantly responsive to human need, physical, mental, or spiritual, wherever it was revealed.

Jesus shared with all who would accept it, *a quality of life permeated by worship*. For him, worship was not an isolated act, perfunctorily performed. Rather, it was the very fiber of his life, every thought, feeling, and act the result of a continuous God-awareness.

These four aspects of Jesus' ministry have been the concern of the redemptive fellowship, the Christian Church, in all ages. Admitting all its tragic failures, it is still true that over the centuries the Church has proclaimed the gospel of Christ, has continued the ministry of teaching and varied service, has nourished a quality of life, individual and corporate, permeated by awareness of God.

These four aspects of Jesus' ministry are still the concern of the Church today—they are equally the concern of the Church-related Christian family.

Recognizing that Jesus deliberately chose the creating of a particular kind of fellowship as the sure method of engendering and sustaining faith, and for the continuation of his ministry to the needs of men, Christian parents, concerned to achieve for themselves and their children a vibrant, joyous Christian faith, will purposefully attempt to follow the same method.

They will strive to live with their children in a genuinely loving fellowship, a fellowship characterized by continuous God-awareness, by patience and mutual forgiveness, by shared concern for neighbors, and by deep joy, the inevitable result of right relations with God and with fellow men. Such a fellowship provides opportunity for each member to achieve his optimal growth, to fulfill his potential as a child of God, a co-worker with him for the redemption of mankind. Parents with these aims in view will relate themselves and their children to the Church, seeking both to give and to receive in that larger body spiritual strengthening and support.

OVERCOMING TENSIONS

The creating of such a Christian family fellowship is a task of Herculean proportions. No one who has ever lived in the midst of a growing family, who has felt the bone-weariness that comes as a result of the twenty-four-hour demands, who has been exposed to the conflicting tensions and the never-ceasing pressures—no one who has experienced these things can be guilty of underestimating the difficulties inherent in such situations.

The incessant labor, the pressures and the tensions, however, exist as an integral part of family living. They exist. They must somehow be lived with and endured. The effort to deal with them *in a Christian framework* does not increase the difficulties. It does not impose an additional task. On the contrary, it is perhaps the only method that holds out any hope for successfully handling family living. The mere effort, although the result falls far short of its potential fruitfulness, lightens burdens, relaxes tensions, and irradiates the whole situation with at least occasional flickers of real joy, and at best with a deep *joie de vivre* that is only temporarily disturbed by surface squalls. In this adventure of purposefully trying to build a Christian family fellowship, times of discouragement and despondency are inevitable. Someone has said, "There are no perfect parents." No one of us even lives up to the best he knows. Each of us fails frequently and abysmally to live out his deep and sincere convictions.

Humanity owes a debt of gratitude to Paul for having seen and expressed so clearly this universal experience:

> For I do not do what I want, but I do the very thing I hate . . .
> I can will what is right, but I cannot do it. For I do not do the
> good I want, but the evil I do not want is what I do. (Romans
> 7:15, 18–19)

Again it is Paul who gives help as to how to handle the inevitable moods of discouragement:

> . . . one thing I do, forgetting what lies behind and straining forward to what lies ahead, I press on toward the goal for the prize of the upward call of God in Christ Jesus. (Philippians 3:13–14)

"Forgetting what lies behind. . . ." Few parents have such great cause for depression as Paul had. How bitterly he must have regretted his persecution of the early Christians! How he must have been haunted by memories of the dying Stephen! And how immeasurably humanity has benefited because he did not wallow in self-denunciation but was able to forget the past!

So parents too need to forget "what lies behind." Recognition of wrongdoing, deep and sincere repentance, are good for the soul. But where self-depreciation continues to the point of interfering with a courageous facing forward, it becomes unwholesome. The surest proof of true repentance is renewed determination and increased effort to do better.

The strength and vitality of spiritual living depend upon constant renewal. In order to "maintain the spiritual glow" no parent can afford to neglect the sources of courage and power that have proved their value for generations of struggling humanity: quiet times of prayer and meditation, frequent and sustained Bible study, participation in the corporate worship of the Church, and in its sacraments.

These are more than pleasant additions to a busy life, to be taken advantage of in occasional moments of comparative leisure. They are the very stuff of Christian living, the essential food without which the spiritual life dries up and expires. You cannot starve your spirit any more than your body without dire consequences. You cannot be a continuous source of spiritual sustenance to your family unless your own spirit is constantly renewed.

The next chapters will consider in some detail the fourfold function of the redemptive fellowship as it is relevant to everyday living in the Christian family.

CHAPTER 3

Interpreting Faith

The previous chapters suggested to parents an approach to
the Christian education of children by the purposeful effort
to create in their own home a loving Christian fellowship,
and by relating the family closely to the larger fellowship of
which it is a part, the Christian Church. They also analyzed
the function of the Christian family, as of the Christian
Church, into four phases of service, based on Jesus' own
ministry: the proclamation of the Gospel, the ministry of
teaching by the spoken word, the ministry of varied service,
and the sharing of a quality of life characterized by continual awareness of God.

This chapter begins the consideration of the meaning of
these four aspects of the family life.

"Jesus came . . . preaching the gospel of God. . . ."
(Mark 1:14) He made a proclamation. It consisted of a
revelation of God's true nature and of God's claim upon his
people. The understanding of the revelation and the acceptance of the claim are the underlying purposes of Christian
education.

The Church has always recognized its responsibility to
proclaim "the good news" and to pronounce God's claim
upon his people. The Christian family, on the other hand,
with few exceptions, has spoken in recent years with a much

less certain voice. Its proclamation has been feeble and waver-
ing. As Paul says:

> If the trumpet give an uncertain sound, who shall prepare him-
> self to the battle? (1 Corinthians 14:8, KJ)

Our modern American civilization is suffering the tragic
effects of the family's "uncertain sound" in the weakening of
moral standards, in sexual excesses, in mounting divorce rates,
in juvenile delinquency, in corruption in high places, in increased mental illness, in racial conflict.

YOU CAN'T LEAVE IT TO THE MINISTER

The parent cannot avoid, even if he wishes to, the necessity
of making some kind of a proclamation to the children, of
interpreting life to them in some ideological framework. If it
seems important that this framework of understanding be in
terms of Christian faith, the proclamation of God's nature,
the presentation of God's claim to love and obedience cannot
safely be left to the minister on Sunday morning. The time
when a proclamation has to be made, when some explanation
of the meaning of life has to be given, is at the moment of
crisis in the family living.

A father loses his job. A pet dies. A rainy day spoils plans
for a long-anticipated picnic. A child asks questions about a
crippled friend. A member of the family or a friend is killed
in an accident. Someone fails in an important examination.
The family has to move to a new location. A newspaper
records a major calamity, a flood or an earthquake. Rumors
of hydrogen bombs and nuclear tests are constant. A man
like Dag Hammarskjold is killed in an airplane accident and
President Kennedy is assassinated. What day passes without
some puzzling fact of life presenting itself for explanation?

What has Christianity to say about these and innumerable
other situations? How proclaim to children in a world filled
with hate and suffering a God of love? How present God's
claim to integrity in a world where so often righteousness and

expediency are unalterably opposed? How achieve for ourselves and for our children the clear-eyed, unshakable faith that can face reality and still proclaim with Paul:

> For I am sure that neither death, nor life, nor angels, nor principalities, nor things present, nor things to come, nor powers, nor height, nor depth, nor anything else in all creation, will be able to separate us from the love of God in Christ Jesus our Lord. (Romans 8:38–39)

The proclamation of the faith must reach beyond the walls of the home. In these days of social upheaval the family is frequently called upon to make a proclamation of its faith to the community.

What is the family attitude on social drinking, on sororities and fraternities in high school and college, on cigarette smoking, on attendance at a civil rights rally, on integration in school and church, on restricted housing, on segregated public facilities such as swimming pools?

Christianity is relevant to each of these social issues and to many more. It has an answer to any problem life can present. It is no easy, sentimental answer. It takes into full account all the obvious evil in the world—in ourselves, and in all men, in all human institutions, and in the Church.

It does not evade the problem of suffering, but staunchly maintains that pain patiently accepted and nobly borne mysteriously results in increased spiritual grace, and exerts an irresistible redemptive influence on the sufferer, and on mankind.

Christianity further proclaims that individual human personality is precious in God's sight, and that it is indestructible, destined for life throughout eternity.

Christianity dares to affirm in spite of the confusing reality of this war-torn world that God is supreme; that love is ultimately the strongest force in the world not excepting the force of nuclear fission; that human relations are unalterably governed by moral law; and that most of the difficulties in which individuals and nations find themselves today are proof that such moral law exists and that it can be ignored or flouted only at the cost of dire consequences. It furthermore proclaims (and this is perhaps its most unique and amazing contribution) that in the midst of sin, suffering, and tragedy, life can be lived joyfully and triumphantly.

This is the proclamation which the redemptive fellowships, the Church and the family, must make. It is a proclamation that can be made only in the midst of life. It must be made repeatedly and consistently, year in and year out. It must be the framework which sustains the family in the midst of crisis. It must be proclaimed and interpreted until its meaning illumines and transforms every day. "Lift up your voice like a trumpet." (Isaiah 58:1)

CHAPTER 4

Teaching by Words

In this chapter the second area of the parents' responsibility, that of teaching by the spoken word, is considered. This is really only an extension of the proclamation of the faith. Much of the proclaiming and the direct teaching must be done in the course of family conversations, often unplanned, unexpected, and frequently inconvenient. It is a little frightening, too, to realize that as parents we are always teaching by every word we say, probably most effectively when we are least aware of it. The offhand comment, the overheard telephone conversation, the hasty, discourteous greeting to a salesman at the door—these all are a part of our teaching.

How unbelievably difficult it is to discipline the tongue, to make hasty, casual comments consistent with our considered beliefs! The Bible describes our predicament in no uncertain terms:

> For we all make many mistakes, and if any one makes no mistakes in what he says he is a perfect man, able to bridle the whole body also. If we put bits into the mouths of horses that they may obey us, we guide their whole bodies. Look at the ships also; though they are so great and are driven by strong winds, they are guided by a very small rudder wherever the will of the pilot directs. So the tongue is a little member and boasts of great things. How great a forest is set ablaze by a small fire!
>
> And the tongue is a fire. The tongue is an unrighteous world among our members, staining the whole body, setting on fire the

cycle of nature, and set on fire by hell. For every kind of beast
and bird, of reptile and sea creature, can be tamed and has been
tamed by humankind, but no human being can tame the tongue
—a restless evil, full of deadly poison. With it we bless the Lord
and Father, and with it we curse men, who are made in the like-
ness of God. From the same mouth come blessing and cursing.
My brethren, this ought not to be so. (James 3:2–10)

In the midst of difficult conversations, prayers from the
Bible may echo in a parent's mind: "Keep watch over the
door of my lips!" (Psalms 141:3) Or "Let the words of my
mouth . . . be acceptable in thy sight." (Psalms 19:14)

No area of conversation is more difficult for the parent
than that of children's questions.[1] Why is it, I used to wonder
wearily, that the youngsters always seem to pick the most
inopportune times to propound questions of tremendous importance? Questions about everyday things around them;
about the inconceivable vastness of the universe; about right
and wrong; about the deep mysteries of birth, and life, and
death, and eternity. What parent is wise enough to answer
rightly the questions of a child? But the questions cannot
remain unanswered. And from the answers he receives the
child is gradually broadening his understanding of the world
in which he lives; is developing his attitudes toward other
people; is finding his way of handling disappointments, con-
troversies, and conflicts; is entering into his Christian heritage,
or is failing so to do.

One area of possible danger in casual conversations needs
special consideration. Many a child's most persistent prejudices come as a direct result of conversations where unchristian ideas are openly expressed or subtly taken for granted.

[1] See the excellent book *When Children Ask,* by Margueritte Harmon
Bro (New York: Harper & Brothers, 1940).

THE THOUGHTLESS REMARK

How often, for instance, do we allow ourselves to slip into a derogatory remark about some individual simply because he belongs to a certain group? "Well, what can you expect of a ———?" Or, "All ———s are like that!" Or, "I never knew a ——— yet who could be trusted." Or, "Don't have anything to do with him—he's a ———."

It is a rare parent who is not occasionally guilty of this kind of carelessness, with the result that seeds of prejudices and antagonisms are planted and nurtured. When remarks of this kind have been made the wise parent is always alert to the need for counteracting them.

"It's never safe to say *all!* We have to think of people as individuals if we want to be fair." Sometimes a true story helps. "Why I knew a ——— once and he wasn't like that at all," etc.

Some parents like to remind children, "You know, there are people, many of them, who are prejudiced against *us*. They think all Americans are money-mad, and drink too much, and drive their cars too fast, and treat people of other races badly. It's most unfair, isn't it? And it is just as unfair for us to decide that we dislike a whole group of people."

Jesus' parable of the Good Samaritan is an excellent bit of Bible material to use in conversations dealing with group animosities. A parent may introduce it with some such statement as this: "You know the Jews and the Samaritans were enemies. They would have nothing to do with each other. They felt about each other just the way you seem to feel about the ———s. Perhaps if Jesus were telling the story today he might tell it about 'a good ———.' It isn't what group a man belongs to that's important. It's what kind of a person he is."

JOKES

One area of family conversation that needs careful watching if prejudicial remarks are to be eliminated is that of jokes.

One lazy summer Saturday afternoon a family and some friends were lolling around in the backyard telling jokes. The mother was busy with mending and was only half listening to the conversation when she suddenly felt something not quite right and looked up quickly. She caught a look of dismay on Margaret's face and realized the cause. One of the family had just told a joke about a certain group, and there, trying to look unself-conscious, sat one of Margaret's best friends—a representative of that particular group.

"I'm thirsty!" said the mother. "Who wants to raid the refrigerator and find us something to drink?"

The joke-telling was successfully interrupted, but the incident was not closed. Later that afternoon when the guests had left, the mother found Margaret in her room, dissolved in tears.

"Oh, Mother!" she sobbed. "Wasn't it awful? I was so ashamed!"

The whole family talked it over. "Gosh, I'm sorry," said the one who had told the joke. "I didn't mean to hurt her— I like her a lot."

"It might have been any one of us," commented the mother. "We're all fond of telling jokes and we've never thought about this before."

"We'll have to be more careful and think about who's around next time," said one of the youngsters.

The father said, "I guess that's not enough. I guess what we have to do is just never tell any joke that might hurt anyone's feelings."

There was a silence. Then, "That's going to cut out an awful lot of jokes," said Ned thoughtfully.

"But Dad's right," said Helen. "Or else we just won't feel safe to bring friends home any more."

And so a thoughtless joke started this family on a long process of self-education. They grew in awareness of the vicious prejudices that can be spread by laughter. They began to look at all jokes with a questioning eye. They listened to jokes with alert minds.

"Now there's a joke that's safe," someone would exclaim. Or, "That's not one for the family to tell!"

Margaret said one day, "I can see what's right to do about telling jokes yourself, but it's harder to know what to do when someone else tells them."

"I know," said Helen. "That still bothers me."

"If you laugh," went on Margaret, "you're sort of approving. And if you say 'I don't think that's funny,' you sound so self-righteous."

"Sometimes you don't have to say anything," said Helen. "You can just not laugh."

"I tried that once," said Margaret, "and they thought I was dumb and started to explain it to me!"

Probably no family will ever find completely satisfactory answers to many of the questions about jokes, but the raising of the questions may in itself be a mark of progress in the direction of human brotherhood, and the effort to find answers may increase the family's sensitivity and their ability to enter sympathetically into the feelings of others.

In addition to a steady awareness of the possible effects of thoughtless remarks, it is helpful to cultivate the habit of consciously applying Christian standards to personal, group, and national conduct. Innumerable family conversations will reflect the parents' efforts along this line.

"You wouldn't like it if someone did that to you," says a parent, "so of course you may not do it to him."

Or, "Of course you're feeling angry and hateful. It's hard not to feel resentful. But sometimes it helps to find out why the other person was so mean. I wonder if . . ."

Or, "You know, something like this happened to me one time. I was so angry! But later I found out . . ."

Or even, "I'm sorry. I didn't mean to sound so cross. I

know when I'm cross at you, it makes you be cross right back again, doesn't it? Let's start over and say what we have to say pleasantly."

Sometimes it will be a news item or a television program that will start a conversation, and the parent may wish to comment, "I wonder if the course our country is following is a truly Christian course, or whether it is based really on expediency."

Children steadily exposed to the influence of consistently applied Christian principles may learn in time to make their own judgments and decisions accordingly.

NO FAITH WITHOUT HONEST DOUBT

Another important difficulty faces parents as they seek to proclaim and teach the Christian faith by the spoken word. It is the need to respect the child's right to his own beliefs and opinions.

A mother was trying earnestly to answer her small daughter's question about God when her fourteen-year-old son broke in almost defiantly, "Sometimes I really wonder whether there *is* any God!"

The mother paused only a moment. Then she said quietly, "But of course you wonder. Everyone does. You'd be a very stupid person if you didn't. People have been wondering about it ever since the first men who lived on earth discovered they had minds with which to think."

The right to doubt and question! No true and satisfying faith was ever achieved without honest doubt. Children's doubts need recognition and encouragement. When children are told "It's wrong to question. You must just have faith!" surely they are not being helped "to love God with all their minds."

One of the most vivid memories of my childhood that has remained with me through the years is of a certain Sunday morning. I was a little girl, perhaps twelve years old. I was sitting in our family pew at a regular Sunday morning service.

Our minister was out of town that day and a stranger was preaching.

"Don't be afraid to ask questions!" he said emphatically in the middle of his sermon. "The Christian religion is not afraid of questions. The truth is never afraid!"

And my twelve-year-old self was caught up in a moment close to ecstasy. I remember I pushed back in the pew and lifted my head with a joyous sense of release, a sudden, breathtaking conviction that it was true! It must be all right to question, to seek explanations and understandings. The truth is never afraid!

That visiting minister went away without knowing that a casual remark of his had resulted in a deeply moving, never-to-be-forgotten religious experience for a little girl sitting quietly in a back pew of the church—an experience that would remain a vivid, shining memory after more than half a century of crowded living.

One other reported conversation between a mother and her six-year-old daughter Ruth is a lovely illustration of what it means to respect the child's right to his own beliefs.

The little girl came in from school one day and exclaimed, "Oh, Mommy, we had the loveliest story in school today— all about a little black sheep that turned white when the baby Jesus put his hand on its head. And it's nicer than a fairy story because it's true. My teacher said so."

The mother hesitated. Then she said carefully, "That is a lovely story, Ruth. It's one of my favorites too. But not every one believes, as your teacher does, that it's true."

Ruth was interested. "Why not?" she wanted to know.

In the long conversation that followed, the mother tried to explain as simply as she could the symbolism of the story. She ended by saying, "So I don't really believe that a black sheep turned white. But I do believe with all my heart that just being with Jesus made dark, ugly, frightening things change. Just being with him made people who had done wrong things want to be kind and loving again. Just being with him made people who had been gloomy and unhappy feel like singing for joy. I think *that's* what the story means."

A long silence ensued. Then Ruth announced, pleasantly but positively, "Well, *I* like to believe *it really happened.*"

The mother's final comment revealed profound respect for a child's freedom to think. "That's all right," she said. "Many people do believe it."

In thinking of the parents' teaching by words, we have given consideration briefly to the need for finding answers to the children's questions, to the danger of developing prejudices through casual remarks and thoughtless jokes, to the wisdom of constantly applying Christian standards to personal, group, and national conduct, and to the necessity of respecting the child's right to his own beliefs.

Easy to do? Of course not. No one ever claimed that the job of being a Christian parent is easy—only that it is challenging, rewarding, worth all the heartache, and the backache, and that it is probably the supremely important job of all human activities, participating as it does in the creative work of God himself.

NOTE: One further responsibility in the area of teaching by the spoken word is often neglected by today's parents—that of making available to the family their rich heritage in the Bible. Because of the basic importance of this responsibility, Part II of this book has been given to a lengthy consideration of the use of the Bible in Christian family living.

CHAPTER 5

Teaching by Deeds

> So Jesus answered them, "My teaching is not mine, but his who sent me; if any man's will is to do his will, he shall know whether the teaching is from God. . . ." (John 7:16–17)

Here in these verses is the recognition that as we "will to do" God's will we grow in our understanding. We learn by doing—an obvious truth, but one the implications of which we often fail to recognize.

A child learns to play the piano by playing it. Skillful guidance is necessary; hearing good music is helpful; but no child learns to play without manipulating the keys.

A boy learns to play baseball, obviously, by playing it. Only as he plays does he gain control of his muscles, co-ordinate eye and hand, grow in his ability to be a team member.

The same principle applies to persons striving to learn to live in Christian ways. Skill comes only as Christian ways of living are persistently followed day after day. And in this very truth lies one of the great difficulties of the parents' task. To live in Christian ways always involves not acts alone but the motives and feelings in back of the acts. A child may be coerced into doing certain things, but his feelings and motives cannot be coerced.

"Tell Grandma you're sorry you were so rude," demands a

well-meaning mother. And a still angry boy mumbles the magic formula, "I'm sorry."

Now sorrow at wrongdoing and wanting to be forgiven are undoubtedly part of Christian living. Neither of these, however, seems to have entered into this boy's heart. And to his original unloving act of rudeness has now been added an untruth.

There is nothing easy or simple about teaching children to live in Christian ways. It cannot be forced. It cannot be imposed from without. It is a matter of inner growth. The parents' task is to provide the opportunity, the encouragement, and, most of all, the contagious example until Christian ways of living become habitual and loved.

Three-year-old Daniel in the very early springtime helped his mother gather bare brown twigs from the forsythia bush in the yard. He helped arrange them in a vase on a sunny window sill. He watched from day to day with intense interest as the brown buds swelled and finally burst open in golden flowers.

Sunday came. "I want to take some flowers to church school," said Daniel.

So his mother carefully drew out a few of the blossoming twigs and gave them to him. Arrived at the church, Daniel trotted up the path and reached the door far ahead of his parents. On the steps of the church stood an elderly lady, a complete stranger to the small boy.

"Oh!" she exclaimed, noticing the flowers in the child's hand, "how lovely!"

Daniel's face broke into a radiant smile. "Would you like to have some?" he asked. And carefully separating some of the twigs from the rest he held them up to her.

Four-year-old Helen woke up early on Christmas morning, and ignoring her bulging stocking, bounced into her parents' room. "Oh, Mommy," she cried, fairly bursting with excitement, *"now* may I give you the present I made for you?"

These are true incidents. How had these two discovered

the joy of giving? The answer is not far to seek. Each had been a part of a family fellowship where over and over again they were provided with opportunities of planning happy surprises for those they loved. Each had been fortunate in having parents who could see behind the crude offerings of the children the love which they were trying to express.

The Christian fellowship, whether in the first century or today, whether it is the Church or the family, is primarily a loving and beloved community. Jesus himself gave priority to the commandments to love God and to love neighbors. (Matthew 22:37–39)

Probably no passage in the New Testament is more familiar or more loved than Paul's famous description of Christian love. Its high idealism is the standard for measuring all Christian human relationships.

> Love is patient and kind; love is not jealous or boastful; it is not arrogant or rude. Love does not insist on its own way; it is not irritable or resentful; it does not rejoice at wrong, but rejoices in the right. Love bears all things, believes all things, hopes all things, endures all things. Love never ends. . . . (1 Corinthians 13:4–8)

No parent could consistently live up to such idealism in the face of the daily stresses and strains, but the value of the standard remains.

One difficulty that stands in the way of the acceptance of love as the rule for life lies in the fact, undeniable and tragic, that offered love is often rudely rejected. Powerful as love is, overcoming at times almost insuperable obstacles, it still remains true that friendly overtures are sometimes rebuked with coldness; that good will is sometimes met with animosity; that outreaching love sometimes encounters malice and hatred.

This is harsh reality. The immature person, child, or adult reacts to an experience of this kind with anger and resentment. It takes a high type of maturity to recognize the risk involved in loving, and to hold fast to love in spite of repeated rebuffs and rejections.

Even Christ's totally self-giving love met temporary defeat and is still rejected by many. The God-given freedom of each individual to accept or reject love carries with it inseparably the risk that the choice may be evil.

Recognizing the risk involved, the parent who is trying to encourage his child to live by the law of love will stand ready to comfort and reassure when necessary. "Never mind—you tried." "The important thing is to hold fast to love even now."

These are wiser responses that the more usual "Oh forget it," or "Well, if that's the way she feels about it, why should you worry?"

An acknowledgment of the possibility of being hurt is no reason for giving up the struggle to live and help the children live in the way of Christian love.

DOES YOUR CHILD KNOW YOU LOVE HIM?

Before they can reach out with love to others children need to know themselves loved. A parent may protest, "Of course I love my child!" That is beside the point. The important thing is: does your child know you love him? Children learn to love by the feel of being loved and by being part of a loving fellowship, with frequent opportunities to learn by actual experience the joy that comes through living in loving ways.

Peter was in kindergarten. Usually he was a friendly, outgoing child, but the time came when his mother became aware that Peter was making frequent unpleasant remarks about Paul. "I don't like Paul. Paul's a nuisance. I wish Paul did not come to kindergarten." And occasionally there were even stronger expressions, "I *hate* Paul."

Things came to a climax when plans were begun for Peter's birthday party. "We'll ask all the boys in your class," suggested Mother.

"All except Paul," said Peter decidedly.

Mother remonstrated gently. "We couldn't leave out just one boy," she said. "That wouldn't be friendly."

"Then I don't want a party," said Peter.

Mother decided it was time to investigate. She visited the kindergarten and found a distracted teacher struggling, so far unsuccessfully, with a situation in which Paul, a newcomer and a most unattractive little boy, was being definitely and unpleasantly rejected by the group. Mother also found out enough about Paul to understand some of the reasons in back of his unlovableness.

At home Mother chose a quiet time for a long talk with Peter. First she told him a story about himself—how she and his father had been so happy when he came; how dearly they had loved him; and later how the three of them had rejoiced when little Dorothy was born; and how lucky they all were to have each other, and to be such a loving family. She talked about how carefully they had chosen a place to live that would be near a fine school, and how glad they were when he, Peter, found so many friends and had such a happy time there. To all of this Peter listened and responded warmly.

"Now I want to tell you another story," said Mother. "Not such a happy story this time." And in carefully chosen phrases she told of another boy, who through no fault of his own had never been a part of a happy family, who now had no father or mother or little sister to love him; a boy who had recently come to live with his grandmother, who was trying to love him enough to make up for the parents he did not have. She said the grandmother had so hoped he would have a happy time in school. But somehow things had not gone right. He had not made friends. The other boys did not like him. They would not let him play with them, and so he was often angry and did mean things to the boys, and of course that just made things worse.

"That's too bad," said Peter, his face serious.

"Yes," said Mother. "It's not a happy story. But I've told you about it because I think perhaps you could help it to have a happier ending."

"Me?" said Peter, opening his eyes wide.

Mother nodded. "You see you know this boy," she said.
Peter shook his head. "I don't know him," he said positively.

"His name is Paul," said Mother.

"Oh!" said Peter.

This was a wise mother. She knew when to stop. She had planted a seed; it would take time for it to grow.

Some three weeks later Mother visited the kindergarten again. She had hardly gotten inside the door before the teacher drew her to one side.

"I've so wanted to see you," she said. "Tell me, did you say anything to Peter about Paul?" Mother admitted that she had.

"I knew it!" exclaimed the teacher. "Why—it's a miracle! He has not only changed his own attitude, he's swung the whole group with him." And she went on to give a detailed account of how one small five-year-old had deliberately set out to show friendliness to an unpopular member of the group with truly astonishing results.

This is not the end of the story; it had a remarkable sequel a year later. Dorothy had been three when all the conversations about Paul took place. A year later she was in nursery school. One day her teacher commented to her mother, "You know, it's a funny thing but all three of us teachers have noticed it and spoken about it. Dorothy seems to be deliberately befriending little Mary. You know she's the retarded child, quite unattractive, really, and most of the children shun her. But Dorothy is always going out of her way to help her."

At home Mother said to Dorothy, "I was glad to hear that you are being friendly to Mary in nursery school."

And amazingly, Dorothy answered, "Well, you know, she's another one like Paul—*she needs an awful lot of loving.*"

Children learn to live in the Christian faith by being part of a loving Christian fellowship characterized by continual God-awareness, by mutual affection, by shared concern for neighbors, and by deep joy.

Children learn to live with Christian love by association with parents who are struggling to achieve Christian love in their relationship to each other, to their children, and to neighbors in the wide meaning of the word.

"Be doers of the word, and not hearers only." (James 1:22)

CHAPTER 6

Teaching by Love

Jesus invariably responded to human need whenever it touched him. The story of his life recorded in the Gospels is a continuing tale of compassion at work. At the beginning of his ministry, in the synagogue at Nazareth, he chose to read these verses from Isaiah. They have been described as his "inaugural address":

> The Spirit of the Lord is upon me,
> because he has anointed me to preach
>   good news to the poor.
> He has sent me to proclaim release to
>   the captives
> and recovering of sight to the blind,
> to set at liberty those who are oppressed,
> to proclaim the acceptable year of the
>   Lord. (Luke 4:18–19)

The proclamation Jesus made by word and deed was twofold. It revealed the true nature of God; it also presented God's claim on his people:

> Love . . . God with all your heart, and with all your soul, and with all your mind, and with all your strength . . . love your neighbor as yourself. (Mark 12:30–31)

He further amplified this claim by other direct teaching. He answered the question "Who is my neighbor?" with one of his unforgettable stories in Luke 10:29–37, the parable of the Good Samaritan. It has frequently been pointed out that the story gives no direct answer to the question. It merely poses another question, "Which . . . *proved neighbor?*" and follows with a directive, "Go and do likewise."

Jesus further left no doubt as to which specific acts could be considered "neighborly."

> . . . for I was hungry and you gave me food, I was thirsty and you gave me drink, I was a stranger and you welcomed me, I was naked and you clothed me, I was sick and you visited me, I was in prison and you came to me . . . as you did it to one of the least of these my brethren, you did it to me. (Matthew 25:35–36, 40)

In the wide field of the ministry of service, the family's first responsibility is to its own members. Loving, thoughtful, day-by-day ministry to each other is the most distinctive mark of the redemptive fellowship. This is not by any means an exclusive ministry of the parents to the children. It begins with the two-way, concerned relationship between husband and wife, each giving to the other the sustaining love and trust that are the essence of Christian marriage. It is a crisscross of relationships from each one to each of the others.

Even the baby in the home has his own special brand of ministry, although at first it is completely unconscious—merely the mysterious response to love, one of the most inexplicable of life's many mysteries. Who has not seen a weary father, burdened by responsibilities and anxieties, suddenly released for a moment from the load of care by a toddler's jubilant welcome, the uplifted hands, the straining arms, the joyous "Daddy! Daddy! Daddy!"

Or what mother at the end of an exhausting day has not felt repaid for hours of labor, for broken rest, for bone-weariness, by a baby's loving, petal-soft hand patting her cheek?

How carefully parents should nurture in children the understanding of ideal Christian family relationships! How patiently in each child must be built up a picture of his particular place in the family group!

"What a thoughtful big sister!" a mother says to an older child who is being gently helpful.

Or, "What a lucky baby to have such a careful big brother!"

Or, "How thankful I am for such willing helpers!"

Such remarks, and an attitude of pleasant expectation, are effective tools in the hands of skillful parents—far more effective than the more usual scolding and nagging, and insistence on acceptable actions without inner motivation.

Fourteen-year-old boys are often considered to be unfeeling, inconsiderate, and irresponsible. One mother reports differently. The father of the family was in the hospital, seriously ill. The mother and the three children sat around the dinner table painfully aware of Dad's empty chair. Four-year-old Mary finished her dinner and went skipping into the living room. She stood on tiptoe and reached up confidently to the corner of the mantel shelf where each evening Dad was accustomed to tuck a package of bonbons or lollipops for an after-dinner treat.

"No candy?" asked Mary.

"No, dear, not tonight," said the mother absent-mindedly. Nothing more was said.

But the next afternoon the mother was in the living room when the older brother came in from school.

"Hi, Mom," he said. "How's Dad?"

"A little more comfortable today," replied his mother. And then looking up she saw that he had just placed on the mantel shelf a package of candies. Never again during the next few weeks did Mary reach up in vain for her after-supper treat.

THE NEED TO FORGIVE

Of course no family will ever achieve perfect relationships. Over and over again peaceful family life will be disrupted by quarreling, by jealousy, by selfishness, by irritability and irresponsibility, and by all the other ailments to which faulty human beings are subject. Over and over again good feelings must be carefully re-established.

The need to forgive and to be forgiven is an essential part of all Christian relationships. How well Jesus knew our human frailty!

> Then Peter came up and said to him, "Lord, how often shall my brother sin against me, and I forgive him? As many as seven times?" Jesus said to him, "I do not say to you seven times, but seventy times seven." (Matthew 18:21–22)

In the intimate family relationships it is inevitable that each will frequently hurt, and in turn be hurt by, the others. It is necessary to grow in the ability to absorb the hurt without lashing back; to forgive with such understanding that the loving relationship is quickly re-established. In this ability to forgive and forget, adults are often put to shame by the children.

Every family looking back over the years could recognize in its own experience numerous instances of the ministry of its members to each other. A husband out of a job, a mother struggling under almost unbearable burdens, a child heartbroken over the death of a pet, a young person facing a major disappointment—these and countless other situations are the times when family love and loyalty count for most.

Two lovely illustrations of this kind of family ministry came to my attention some years ago, both from the same family, a three-generation family in which Grandma, close to ninety, had been bedridden for over a year, crippled with arthritis.

One day teen-age Julia came downstairs from Grandma's room where she had been reading out loud.

"It must be awful, just to lie there all day long and *do nothing!*" she exclaimed. "My throat hurts," she added.

"I know," answered the mother. "Grandma's hearing has been very bad the last few days."

"Isn't there *anything* she can do?" persisted Julia.

"I haven't been able to think of much," answered the

mother. "Even with earphones she can't understand the radio. She listens to music once in a while. And she turns over the pages of a magazine, but I don't think she can see any but the largest pictures. She does love to talk—just sitting and listening to her is about the kindest thing we can do, I guess."

A day or two later Julia came in with a package. "Look," she said, "I got a pair of large-size knitting needles and some heavy wool. I can knit without looking at the stitches. Maybe Grandma can learn too."

Julia's plan worked better than might have been expected. Fumblingly, Grandma's arthritic hands manipulated the needles. At night after Grandma was settled, Julia would stealthily bring out the knitting bag, pick up the dropped stitches, and straighten out the snarls. Sometimes it meant ripping out and reknitting all that Grandma had done.

"She'll never be able to do it," Julia decided sadly.

But her mother reassured her. "As long as she thinks she can it's all right," she said. "It's already accomplished what you wanted—it keeps her busy and helps pass the weary hours."

The second incident occurred in the same family, some months later. This time it was the mother herself who was the recipient of the loving family ministry.

Like many elderly people Grandma was usually restless during the night. Often the mother would be up three or four times between midnight and dawn. Then just when the family were getting up Grandma would settle down for her best sleep.

Christmas came. The house was full of the spicy fragrance of evergreens. On Christmas morning the family gathered around Grandma's bed to watch her open her presents. Grandma exclaimed with delight over each package and then, weary, settled back against her pillows for a rest while the family moved down to the living room to open presents in front of the fire blazing on the hearth. When the last package under the tree had been opened, the father brought out one more.

"This is for you," he said, handing it to the mother, "from the family."

With great curiosity the mother unwrapped the box, opened it, and reached inside. A small pitcher and sugar bowl came first, then a cup and saucer, a plate, and an individual coffee pot. She looked up puzzled. "They're very pretty," she said.

"Part of the present can't be wrapped up," explained her husband. "From now on, the family gets their own breakfast and you get yours—in bed when we're ready to leave the house."

The mother looked from her new breakfast set to the loving faces of her family. "You don't know what that will mean!" she exclaimed fervently.

Speaking of the experience years later, the mother commented, "Oh, the blessedness of those extra minutes of sleep each morning! Vaguely, I'd hear the alarm clock go off and feel my husband's quick move to shut it off. Then he'd tuck the covers around me and tiptoe out to call the rest of the family. Oh, the indescribable luxury of not having to move! I'd sink back into deep, relaxed sleep. An indefinite time later the smell of coffee would penetrate my slumbers and there would be one of the girls beside me with my tray set with my special breakfast dishes."

How humbly grateful each of us must be who knows at first hand the unspeakable blessing of family love! Surely we can never deserve the countless small ministries that we accept day after day from those in our home. Small they may be, but Jesus himself said that even the giving of a cup of cold water in the right spirit was important. (Matthew 10:42 and Mark 9:41) The loving ministry within the family group is characteristic of the redemptive fellowship.

CHAPTER 7

Teaching to Share

> Above all hold unfailing your love for one another. . . . Practice hospitality ungrudgingly. . . . As each has received a gift, employ it for one another, as good stewards of God's varied grace. (1 Peter 4:8–10)

What a charter for a family striving to be Christian! What has "God's varied grace" provided *your* family? Have you been given good health, a comfortable home, a reasonably adequate income?

What about special "gifts" your family has received? Does someone have a lovely expressive voice, or skill and training as a pianist or violinist? Is someone specially gifted in art?

Does someone have a flair for handling babies? Or for communicating with teen-agers? Or for establishing warm relationships with lonely elderly people?

Is someone an extra-special cook? Is someone skilled in the use of tools? Does someone have a rare gift of making friends? Or of spreading a warm cordiality in a group?

If all the family has and is could be seen as evidence of "God's varied grace," if every special gift could be similarly regarded, and if the family could consciously accept their responsibility as "stewards," what an indescribably rich and effective ministry a combined family could offer!

The family that is learning the ministry of service *within* the home will inevitably find its ministry overflowing in innumerable channels *outside* the home.

A new family moves into the neighborhood. Perhaps Mother sends in a fresh-baked cake for supper.

A neighbor's child is sick. A boy next door may go to the drugstore for a prescription.

A neighbor's child has an accident and is rushed to the hospital. Other children in the family need to be cared for.

A death occurs in a neighbor's family. How precious at such a time are the loving ministries of friends!

A family of a minority group moves into a home nearby. What is a Christian family's responsibility toward them?

Wise parents include the children in considering how to meet these frequently presented needs, and watch for opportunities for the children to share in the ministry. "This is what has happened. I wonder how our family may help?"

The other side of the picture is also important. The development of appreciation for all that neighbors do for us needs to be cultivated.

One family has developed a delightful tradition as a part of their celebration of Thanksgiving each year. They send "we are thankful *for you*" cards or gifts to neighbors and friends for whom they feel especially grateful. For this family Thanksgiving has come to be more than a day for a big turkey dinner.

So far the family's ministry of service has been considered as it functions within the family and to a close circle of friends or neighbors. Today no home is so isolated as to escape confrontation by human needs on a wider basis than that of immediate neighbors.

Red feather, community chest appeals, Red Cross catastrophe relief, drives for support of medical research, for aid to the handicapped—all these are publicized through mailings, through newspapers and magazines, through radio and television.

The attitude of the parents toward these appeals is observed by the children and will color their own giving for years to come. Are all such appeals dropped into the scrap-basket? Are they obviously a source of annoyance? Are they ever seriously considered as part of a family's carefully thought-out plan of giving?

"How can anyone possibly give to everything?" a parent may exclaim impatiently. "And besides, how can you tell the genuine appeal from the racket?"

GIVING MUST BE PLANNED

What is being suggested here is not indiscriminate and unintelligent giving. On the contrary. Planned giving (planned whenever possible by the whole family) is prompted by the deep desire to respond to as many human needs as possible. It recognizes the truth that all things come from God, and of his own have we given in his service. (See 1 Chronicles 29:14) It accepts God's claim to the whole of our lives and our possessions. It embodies the idea of stewardship and of neighborliness in active service. It recognizes the claim of human need in many and diverse forms—in forms as varied as God's grace to us.

The parents' responsibility in this area is not just to be good stewards themselves; it is also to train the children to be good stewards. Here again it is the inner motives and feelings that are important. It is not enough to insist that a child "give" a percentage of his allowance. The aim is warm-hearted response to human need.

Fortunately this is one area where concerned parents find little difficulty. Normal, happy children almost always respond with warmth to any need presented to them. Frequently they are the ones who represent the need to their parents!

Allen, a twelve-year-old, came home from school one day in a thoughtful mood. He fidgeted around the room, twiddled with the television set, and finally flung himself into a chair.

"Mom," he said, "there's a picture on the bus—you know, one of the advertising cards. It says 'Hunger Hurts,' and it shows a hungry child with an empty cup." His mother nodded. "I've seen it," she said gravely.

"Well," said the boy, "can I send a dollar of my allowance to them?"

"Of course," agreed his mother. "And I'll add another dollar to it."

For children, giving makes most sense when it is closely related to the experiences of every day. A new coat replaces one that has been outgrown. The outgrown coat could make some child deeply grateful.

A new pair of shoes may be the occasion of a small donation to help buy shoes for some needy person. One family keeps a baby shoe on the sideboard and each member of the family drops in a thank offering whenever new shoes are bought. When the shoe is filled, the money is given to a director of a nursery, who always knows just where a new pair of shoes is most needed.

A child is sick and recovers. A "thank offering" to a local or missionary hospital is appropriate. A very special gift from the family (a growing plant, perhaps) is sent to some shut-in friend who will *not* get well again.

A child learns to read and is caught up with the excitement of this new accomplishment. Now he might well be introduced to the work of the World Literacy Campaign, or to the amazing work of the American Bible Society, which has been instrumental in publishing parts of our Bible in over 1100 languages.

The red and black star of the American Friends Service Committee is known the world over. This organization has a unique record for planning projects for giving that have strong appeal for children. Every concerned family intent on meeting human needs should be familiar with the work of this group.

The United Nations is in ill repute in some quarters because of its failure so far to solve all the apparently insoluble problems of international relations. It has, however, a number of achievements to its credit, none quite so spectacular, perhaps, as the transformation of Halloween from a mere fun night of begging into a tremendous, co-operative enterprise to provide funds for ministry to hungry and sick children around the world. In 1962 the amount collected was $2,000,000. The United Nations International Children's Fund (UNICEF) deserves the enthusiastic support of all people of good will and its work should most certainly be a subject of occasional discussion and continuing support in Church-related families.

The American Foundation for the Blind and the John Milton Society do outstanding work in many areas of need: in rehabilitating and training blind workers, in educating blind children, in providing "talking books," and volumes of Braille, and so forth.

When a child first comes in contact with a blind person he should become informed about this service and be given an opportunity to share in this ministry.[1]

Many families have "adopted" a child through the Christian Children's Fund and have found the exchange of letters a fascinating family experience.

The list could be indefinitely extended. Jesus responded to human needs of many kinds, to physical, mental, emotional, and spiritual needs. Parents will be concerned to share with their children a similar many-sided response, "as good stewards of God's varied grace."

A Church-related family will want to channel much of its giving through the benevolent program of its local church.

The giving of the regular weekly offering has been made more significant to some families by a simple home ritual of preparation at some convenient time, usually on Saturday evening.

At the selected time, one of the parents reminds the children of some of the needs the offering is designed to meet. Then all the offering envelopes for the next day are filled.

[1] An excellent book which presents the story of a blind child wholesomely and not sentimentally is *Windows for Rosemary*, by Marguerite Vance (New York: E. P. Dutton & Company, Inc., 1956).

The family read or recite in unison an appropriate Bible verse such as one of the following:

> Take from among you an offering to the Lord; whoever is of a generous heart, let him bring the Lord's offering. (Exodus 35:5)

> For all things come from thee, and of thy own have we given thee. (1 Chronicles 29:14)

> As each has received a gift, employ it for one another, as good stewards of God's varied grace. (1 Peter 4:10)

Opportunities for the discussion of the meaning of the verses will occur, and the whole idea of Christian stewardship will gradually become clear.

The simple ritual may close with a brief prayer for God's blessing on the Church, and a petition that each member of the family may help the prayer to be answered.

In many families thoughtful consideration is given to the occasional "special appeals" sent home by the church (such as the One Great Hour of Sharing) and the parents see to it that they are sufficiently informed about such agencies as Church World Service and denominational projects to answer the children's questions intelligently.

The thoughtful and regular sharing of income is, however, not the only claim the Church makes on its families. According to the varied gifts God has given, each member is called upon to do his share in the redemptive fellowship of the Church. The minister is not "the Church," and he cannot possibly carry on an effective ministry unless he has the warm co-operative support of dozens of loyal dedicated workers.

In the light of these understandings, in countless churches across the land, members of Christian families offer humbly to God their gifts of service in his Church, contributing hours of labor in the kitchen, volunteering for clerical work in the office, doing parish visiting, teaching in the Church School, leading youth groups, serving on committees, singing in the choir, serving as ushers, deacons, trustees.

Not all Church-related families accept their full responsibility for the use of their talents in the Church. Too many are like the woman quoted by Margueritte Harmon Bro, "All I wants is to be a bencher with no compelments."[2]

"Benchers with no compelments" are what too many church members aim to be! Too many are content to sit back and receive whatever the Church may offer, feeling free, of course, to criticize harshly everything that is attempted by those few with inconvenient "compelments" who do the work. But of course it is a strange fact, readily observable, that the vast spiritual resources of the Church are available only to those who enter into the fellowship with wholehearted commitment.

The family truly seeking to bear its share of responsibility in the work of the Church will have plenty of "compelments." To be part of the body of Christ at work in the world is a daring challenge. It is also a richly rewarding adventure.

[2] *Every Day a Prayer* (New York: Harper & Brothers, 1943), p. 152.

CHAPTER 8

Family Worship

Previous chapters have considered Jesus' proclamation, his ministry of teaching, and his ministry of service, and the parallel responsibilities for Christian families today.

The fourth element of Jesus' total ministry to the needs of people was his sharing of a quality of life marked by continual God-awareness. If the redemptive fellowships of the Christian Church and home are to move toward an approximation of the original fellowship of Jesus and his disciples, it will be necessary once again to capture the God-consciousness that permeates and redeems everyday living.

A generation ago "family worship" had unpleasant connotations for many people. It recalled, sometimes, long and boring interludes in the exciting business of living, with father or grandfather reading interminable chapters from the Bible, some of which were completely incomprehensible to small listeners, followed by equally lengthy prayers, before the final and welcome "Amen" released the "captive audience" to more enjoyable occupations.

Few of today's young parents have any such memories. The suggestion of family worship is apt to be met by them with embarrassment, and an initial resistance that seems sometimes to grow out of an unwillingness to pretend that they are better than they are!

When I was a little girl, the home in which I lived was

lighted by candles and oil lamps. I remember quite clearly one day when some large cartons were opened with much excitement and some new and much-improved "Angle oil lamps" were unpacked and installed. These lamps hung from the ceiling and had three separate wicks fed from a single reservoir of oil. Years later the Angle lamps were replaced by gas fixtures. Still later the gas fixtures were discarded and electric fixtures took their place.

In turn we discarded candles, oil lamps, Angle lamps, and gas lights. But we did not throw out out-moded lights and grope around in the darkness. We replaced each one with something better.

The old type of family worship proved in many instances inadequate to the demands of modern living. It was discarded, perhaps wisely. *But what have you put in its place?* The purpose of family worship was to root the family living in eternal verities. How are you accomplishing this purpose today?

No single area of religious life needs such creative, adventurous exploring as that of worship in the family. Discard, if it seems wise to you, old forms and old semantics. Call it what you like; use old forms or find or create new ones. But somehow, in the midst of your crowded family living, make room for the purposeful cultivation and conservation of Christian values, which is the aim and the result of all true worship.

At the heart of worship is prayer.

> Of all the things the world now desperately needs [Georgia Harkness says], none is more needed than an upsurge of vital, God-centered, intelligently grounded prayer.[1]

She goes on to list a number of other much-needed things such as: a new international order, control of atomic energy for constructive purposes, more understanding and justice between labor and management, the end of poverty and hunger,

[1] *Prayer and the Common Life* (Nashville: Abingdon-Cokesbury Press, 1948), p. 13.

and so on. And then she reiterates her previous statement, "Nothing is more needed than a general upsurge of the right kind of prayer."

That is a thought-provoking statement, and some, I am sure, will question its validity. To many people today, prayer is a lost art.

"It doesn't make sense," someone will say. "God isn't going to be coaxed into changing anything just because I ask him to. And besides, maybe someone else is praying to him for just the opposite thing. For example, in a war, when both sides are praying for victory. He can't possibly grant both prayers."

Such comments reveal a woeful lack of understanding of "vital, God-centered, intelligently grounded" prayer. Because the point of view expressed is still fairly prevalent, it may be helpful to state quite positively and simply what genuine prayer is *not*. It is not asking God for special favors or for preferential treatment. It is not advising God or trying to dictate to him how to run his universe.

Dr. Fosdick has made an interesting study of recorded prayers in the Bible.[2] He points out that prayer in primitive religion always involves the effort to persuade a god to do man's will, and that many Old Testament prayers are on this level. In the New Testament, however, prayer is most frequently an expression of the desire to "realize the sustaining power" of God.

To be effective for such a purpose, prayer must be an opening of the heart to God, a turning toward him in expectancy, a waiting for the welling-up of his spirit within the heart, a "tuning-in" of the mind in order to receive what God is ready to communicate.

This seems to have been what prayer was to Jesus.

> And in the morning, a great while before day, he rose and went out to a lonely place, and there he prayed. (Mark 1:35)

[2] Harry Emerson Fosdick, *A Guide to Understanding the Bible* (New York: Harper & Row, Publishers, Incorporated). See Chapter V, "The Idea of Fellowship with God."

It is interesting to note that at the very beginning and again near the very end of Jesus' public ministry there were similar withdrawals for prayer—the forty days in the Wilderness and the lonely vigil in Gethsemane. Between these two are scattered instances indicating that prayer and meditation were an important part of his busy days.

That these habitual periods of withdrawal were fruitful, that Jesus came back from them renewed and invigorated, was clearly recognized by the disciples.

"Lord, teach us to pray," (Luke 11:1) one of them demanded one day. What an astonishing request! For the disciples were all Jews. From early childhood they had been trained in the frequent ritualistic repetition of prayers. How doubly significant, therefore, was the demand, "Lord, teach us to pray"! What they were really asking was, "Teach us to pray *as you do,* so that we may channel into our lives the infinite power of almighty God."

TIME FOR WITHDRAWAL

As parents, we need to strive earnestly for more periods of withdrawal, to look at the whole of our lives objectively, to evaluate our daily living, to secure a God-given sense of direction. The "lonely place," the fenced-in corner of time and space for quiet meditation and prayer, never can be achieved without effort. (Let us not underestimate the value of the regular weekly Church services for this purpose.)

In our effort to achieve this habitual time for peaceful thinking, let us not fail to recognize the inestimable value of frequent mental withdrawals even in the midst of daily activities. Think for a moment of the hours spent (and often wasted) by fathers in commuting or in driving alone. Think of the hours mothers spend at countless physical tasks that keep their hands busy but leave their minds free. Here are "lonely places" ready to be used, waiting to be filled with the renewal of spiritual strength and power from the unseen but always available source.

Some parents, having already established habits of prayer according to their own need and their own liking, may find unnecessary any further help as to how to pray. Others, who may have failed to establish any such custom, or who find it difficult to "maintain the spiritual glow" in their prayer life, may welcome guidance in practical ways of starting or deepening the values of personal prayer. It seems, moreover, obviously true that only as parents do learn the reality and fruitfulness of genuine prayer will they be able gradually to share their own discoveries with their children.

Surely no one could attempt to give guidance in this important area of Christian experience without a deep feeling of humility; and no one could hope that any advice given could work equally well for all parents. Moreover, any suggestions offered here should be thought of as merely a beginning, a way perhaps to get started on a long and personal endeavor to experience more deeply and continuously God's sustaining companionship.

As one approaches any moment of informal or formal prayer, one thought ought to be held firmly in the heart. It is not in reality we who are calling upon God to answer us. The reverse is true: God has initiated the contact. He has called us, and we are answering his call:

> Behold, I stand at the door and knock; if any one hears my voice and opens the door, I will come in to him. . . . (Revelation 3:20)

The sincerity or efficacy of a prayer is never to be judged by its length. Jesus said:

> And in praying do not heap up empty phrases as the Gentiles do; for they think that they will be heard for their many words. (Matthew 6:7)

It was at this time that Jesus gave his disciples that brief prayer of fifty-four words through which millions of people continue to lift up their hearts to God. (Matthew 6:9–13)

Far more important than the length of prayers is their frequency. It is hoped that parents, by following some of the procedures described in the next chapter, and by inventing new devices of their own, may learn (and help their children learn) the efficacy of frequent, hidden-in-the-heart prayers, prayers right in the midst of life's crowded moments, prayers by which it may truly be possible to train oneself to "pray without ceasing." (1 Thessalonians 5:17, KJ)

CHAPTER 9

Family Prayer

This chapter deals with four daily times for prayer: in the morning, during the day, at meal times, and in the evening. In each section appropriate Bible prayer verses are suggested. The use of Bible prayers is not meant to be a substitute for the spontaneous outpourings of a parent's own prayers. It is meant rather to stimulate and encourage such personal experiences by providing patterns and a rich language of worship. Merely to repeat these Bible verses, moreover, is not necessarily to pray. Only as a person chooses those passages which truly express his own feelings, and uses them as though they were being said for the first time, only so will they be for him true worship.

PRAYER IN THE MORNING

Those who have mastered the art of effective prayer stress the importance of centering the first waking thoughts on God. This need not be a long and extended period of prayer. A few seconds is enough to set the tone for the day's activities.

In preparation for this morning moment, search in the Bible, particularly in the Psalms, for prayer verses, or prayer-mood verses to use in this way as a reminder that *God is*. Use the same verse or passage repeatedly until it has sunk into your consciousness and become a permanent part of your language of worship.

As a help in memorizing, you may like to copy on cards several of the selections you have chosen. These cards may stand on the table by your bed as a reminder, until you have established the habit of this morning moment of prayer. Cards about 5"×9" are a good size. They may be folded in half to stand up like tents. Print a selection on each side of the tent, then turn it inside out and print two more.

Perhaps some of the passages below speak to your need.

Lord, thou has been our dwelling place
   in all generations.
Before the mountains were brought forth,
   or ever thou hadst formed the earth and the world,
   from everlasting to everlasting thou art God.
                       PSALMS 90:1–2

This is the day which the Lord has made;
   let us rejoice and be glad in it.
                  PSALMS 118:24

Satisfy us in the morning with thy steadfast love,
   that we may rejoice and be glad all our days.
                  PSALMS 90:14

Teach me thy way, O Lord,
   that I may walk in thy truth. . . .
                  PSALMS 86:11

Let me hear what God the Lord will speak. . . .
                  PSALMS 85:8

So teach us to number our days
   that we may get a heart of wisdom.
                  PSALMS 90:12

Search me, O God, and know my heart!
   Try me and know my thoughts!
And see if there be any wicked way in me,
   and lead me in the way everlasting!
                  PSALMS 139:23–24

Two or three longer passages seem particularly appropriate for morning thoughts:

> Bless the Lord, O my soul;
>> and all that is within me, bless his holy name!
>
> Bless the Lord, O my soul,
>> and forget not all his benefits,
>
> who forgives all your iniquity,
>> who heals all your diseases,
>
> who redeems your life from the Pit,
>> who crowns you with steadfast love and mercy,
>
> who satisfies you with good as long as you live
>> so that your youth is renewed like the eagle's.
>
> PSALMS 103:1–5

> Have you not known? Have you not heard?
> The Lord is the everlasting God,
>> the Creator of the ends of the earth.
>
> He does not faint or grow weary,
>> his understanding is unsearchable.
>
> He gives power to the faint,
>> and to him who has no might he increases strength.
>
> Even youths shall faint and be weary,
>> and young men shall fall exhausted;
>
> but they who wait for the Lord shall renew their strength,
>> they shall mount up with wings like eagles,
>
> they shall run and not be weary,
>> they shall walk and not faint.
>
> ISAIAH 40:28–31

> Seek the Lord while he may be found,
>> call upon him while he is near;
>
> let the wicked forsake his way,
>> and the unrighteous man his thoughts;
>
> let him return to the Lord, that he may have mercy on him,
>> and to our God, for he will abundantly pardon.
>
> For my thoughts are not your thoughts,
>> neither are your ways my ways, says the Lord.
>
> For as the heavens are higher than the earth,
>> so are my ways higher than your ways
>> and my thoughts than your thoughts.
>
> ISAIAH 55:6–9

Whither shall I go from thy Spirit?
  Or whither shall I flee from thy presence?
If I ascend to heaven, thou art there!
  If I make my bed in Sheol, thou art there!
If I take the wings of the morning
  and dwell in the uttermost parts of the sea,
even there thy hand shall lead me,
  and thy right hand shall hold me.
If I say, "Let only darkness cover me,
  and the light about me be night,"
even the darkness is not dark to thee,
  the night is bright as the day;
  for darkness is as light with thee.

PSALMS 139:7–12

PRAYER DURING THE DAY

Choose certain "reminders" of Jesus' teachings and start training yourself to brief but fruitful *flash memories* or *flash prayers* at frequent intervals throughout the day.

Jesus often used this method of making everyday things around him the symbols of his spiritual teachings.

> "You are the *salt* of the earth" (Matthew 5:13). "You are the *light* of the world" (Matthew 5:14). "Look at the *birds* of the air" (Matthew 6:26). "Consider the *lilies* of the field" (Matthew 6:28). "The *house* on the rock" (Matthew 7:24–25). "Are not *two sparrows* sold for a penny?" (Matthew 10:29). "He makes his *sun* rise on the evil and on the good, and sends *rain* on the just and on the unjust" (Matthew 5:45). "The kingdom of heaven is like *leaven*" (Matthew 13:33), and "like a grain of mustard *seed*" (Matthew 13:31). "I am the *bread* of life" (John 6:35). "If a man has a hundred *sheep*" (Matthew 18:12). The *bread* and the *wine* (Matthew 26:26–28).

So we today can keep alive in our hearts and minds some of Jesus' teachings by associating them persistently and repeatedly with the "homely things" around us. How true is the insight that Edwin Markham caught in his poem *The Consecration of the Common Way,* from which these lines are taken:

The King of Heaven had come our way,
And in a lowly stable lay: . . .
His palace was a wayside shed,
A battered manger was his bed;
An ox and ass with breathings deep
Made warm the chamber of his sleep.

Three sparrows with a friendly sound
Were picking barley from the ground:
An early sunbeam, long and thin,
Slanted across the dark within,
And brightened in its silver fall
A cart-wheel leaning to the wall.
An ox-yoke hung upon a hook;
A worn plow with a clumsy crook
Was lying idly by the wheel.
And everywhere there was the feel
Of that sweet peace that labor brings—
The peace that dwells with homely things.

Now have the homely things been made
Sacred, and a glory on them laid.
For He whose shelter was a stall,
The King, was born among them all.
He came to handle saw and plane,
To use and hallow the profane:
Now is the holy not afar
In temples lighted by a star,
But where the loves and labors are.
Now that the King has gone this way,
Great are the things of every day![1]

"Now is the holy not afar" but close at hand in our homes "where the loves and labors are." How has Jesus hallowed the "homely things"? Surely by connecting with them the deep insights of religion. Can we purposefully increase our own understanding of how "great are the things of every day" by using them as constant reminders of the values we are trying to incarnate in our family living?

Suppose, for instance, that a mother trained herself to have a *flash memory* every time she picked up a salt cellar: "You

[1] Reprinted by permission of Virgil Markham.

are the salt of the earth." How could she fail to ask herself each time, "Is the flavor I am adding to the family life now, this minute, a truly Christian flavor?"

Suppose a father trained himself to have a *flash memory* every time he touched a light switch: "You are the light of the world." Could he fail to wonder, "Am I truly a light to my family? Is the home brighter, more cheerful, more truly Christian because I am here? Are the children really being enlightened by my words and by my actions? Or am I adding to their confusion?"

Suppose every time parents felt the welcome warmth of the sun they had a *flash memory:* "He makes his sun to rise on the evil and the good." How could they fail to ask, "Is our love for each other, and for the children, like that—steady, dependable, life-giving?"

Suppose every time we saw sparrows we had a *flash memory:* "Not one of them will fall to the ground without your Father's will. . . . Fear not, therefore, you are of more value than many sparrows." Of value—to God! Would we not lift up our heads and straighten our shoulders, and carry the daily load a bit more easily inspired by that thought?

Such moments are truly prayer moments, though no words of prayer may be formulated.

Another suggestion for prayer during the day is to make it a practice to lift your mind and heart to God frequently, as various situations arise.

> Little prayers of a single sentence in the midst of things— petitions for help to do the work right, joyous thanksgiving, a plea for forgiveness, commitment to God to go forward without worrying over what is ahead or what has already happened—such prayers can make the day over from monotony or defeat to triumph . . . Little silent thrusts of prayer throughout the waking hours, in work or leisure, can so shape the tenor of one's spirit that it is possible to live serenely and zestfully in the midst of whatever comes.[2]

[2] Georgia Harkness, *Prayer and the Common Life* (Nashville: Abingdon-Cokesbury Press, 1948), pp. 129–30.

Most of these "thrusts of prayer" will find their own words growing out of the situations. But the true lover of the Bible finds prayers from its pages coming easily to his lips.

> In thy presence there is fullness of joy.
> PSALMS 16:11

> I fear no evil; for thou art with me.
> PSALMS 23:4

> Who can discern his errors?
>   Clear thou me from hidden faults.
> PSALMS 19:12

> Thou holdest my lot.
> The lines have fallen for me in pleasant places.
> PSALMS 16:5, 6

> Let the words of my mouth and the meditation of my heart
>   be acceptable in thy sight,
> O Lord. . . .
>   PSALMS 19:14

> When I am afraid, I put my trust in thee.
> PSALMS 56:3

> Teach me thy way, O Lord,
>   that I may walk in thy truth.
> PSALMS 86:11

> Set a guard over my mouth, O Lord,
>   keep watch over the door of my lips!
> PSALMS 141:3

> Teach me to do thy will. . . .
> PSALMS 143:10

> May Christ dwell in my heart, so that I may be rooted and
> grounded in love.
>   See EPHESIANS 3:17

> Father, forgive them—
>   LUKE 23:34

The mood of constant prayer is beautifully expressed in the Negro spiritual:

> *Every time I feel the Spirit*
> *Moving in my heart*
> *I will pray.*

PRAYER AT MEAL TIMES

The custom of grace at table has persisted in many homes where it is the only form of worship in which the family join. Its inadequacies are obvious; it very easily degenerates into a meaningless routine that is uninspired and even irreverent. *But it need not.*

One way to avoid this is to take advantage of lovely Bible verses that adequately express the gratitude of the human heart. It will be helpful if these are typed or printed on cards, although parents should be careful that children know they are from the Bible. These verses may be used in a variety of ways. Children may take turns in choosing and repeating one; or a selected verse may be repeated in unison. Or each member of the family may choose one, and the verses may be read in turn.

One family with Quaker leanings often have a silent grace, the family joining hands around the table. Another family like to sing grace occasionally, and have found several appropriate hymns they use in this way.

Children often enjoy making up an original tune for a Bible verse, and if this is done they enter into the grace with new understanding and enjoyment. Some musical families may enjoy chanting one of the brief verses. This may even be done very simply in parts. The father may chant, for instance, "We give thanks to thee, O God" (Psalms 75:1), on the first note of the scale. The children may then chant the words on the third note; the mother following on the fifth, and concluding with all singing together in harmony. This makes a really lovely and unusual grace.

A few verses appropriate for grace are given below. Watch for others as you read the Bible:

> O give thanks to the Lord, for he is good;
> for his steadfast love endures for ever!
> PSALMS 106:1

The Lord hath done great things for us; whereof
we are glad.
PSALMS 126:3, KJ

This is the day which the Lord has made;
let us rejoice and be glad in it.
PSALMS 118:24

I will give thanks to the Lord with my whole heart.
PSALMS 9:1

Thou, O Lord, hast made me glad by thy work:
at the works of thy hands I sing for joy.
PSALMS 92:4

The steadfast love of the Lord is from everlasting
to everlasting.
PSALMS 103:17

O Lord, how manifold are thy works!
In wisdom hast thou made them all.
PSALMS 104:24

I will sing to the Lord as long as I live.
PSALMS 104:33

We give thanks to thee, O God; we give thanks.
PSALMS 75:1

PRAYER IN THE EVENING

The beginning and the end of the day seem to be especially
appropriate times for prayer. At night when the day's work
is ended, a temptation sometimes comes to sink down into
self-pity, to go over the disappointments and failures of the
day, to brood over small hurts until they become exaggerated
out of all proportion to their real significance. Then each of
us needs to follow the Psalmist's advice:

Bless the Lord, O my soul,
and forget not all his benefits.
PSALMS 103:2

A concentration of our minds on the things for which we
are truly grateful will nearly always lift us above self-centered

narrowness and pettiness. Moreover, counting our blessings is one sure way of discovering in ourselves those faults and failings which have hindered the full blossoming of Christian family life.

The evening prayer seems naturally to fall into three parts: thanksgiving, confession, recommitment to what is highest and best. After these, how comforting to put all thoughts out of the mind save a reassuring recollection of God's steadfast love!

The parent who has memorized some of the great, inspired passages of the Bible can lie still in the quiet darkness, with eyes closed, while the comforting words bring their ministry of peace to the tired body and spirit.

For many the Twenty-third Psalm will be a favorite. Others may choose Psalms twenty-four, eight, nineteen, one hundred twenty-one. Other comforting passages are:

> God is our refuge and strength,
>   a very present help in trouble.
> Therefore we will not fear though the earth should change,
>   though the mountains shake in the heart of the sea;
> though its waters roar and foam,
>   though the mountains tremble with its tumult.
>   PSALMS 46:1–3

> For the Lord is a great God,
>   and a great King above all gods.
> In his hand are the depths of the earth;
>   the heights of the mountains are his also.
> The sea is his, for he made it,
>   for his hands formed the dry land.
>
> O come, let us worship and bow down,
>   let us kneel before the Lord, our Maker!
> For he is our God,
>   and we are the people of his pasture,
>   and the sheep of his hand.
>   PSALMS 95:3–7

O Lord, thou hast searched me and known me!
Thou knowest when I sit down and when I rise up;
  thou discernest my thoughts from afar.
Thou searchest out my path and my lying down,
  and art acquainted with all my ways.

Even before a word is on my tongue,
  lo, O Lord, thou knowest it altogether.
Thou dost beset me behind and before,
  and layest thy hand upon me.
Such knowledge is too wonderful for me,
  it is high, I cannot attain it.

PSALMS 139:1–6

The suggestions given above are simple enough to be used by children as well as parents. It is easy to imagine a child questioning a parent about a "tent" of prayer verses standing on a bedside table. Perhaps the parent explains simply, "Each morning Dad and I read one of these verses to remind us of God's loving care." It would not be at all surprising, if the child spontaneously suggests, "I want one, too."

It is easy to imagine a parent saying to a child scattering crumbs for birds, "Whenever I see the little sparrows I like to remember what Jesus said about them." (Matthew 10:29)

In such completely natural ways parents may share with children a way of prayer that has first become familiar and helpful to them, and together the family may increase their awareness of God in the midst of daily living.

CONCLUSION

The previous chapters have been concerned with presenting the Christian family at its best as a redemptive fellowship, "the Church in thy house." An effort has been made to show that the Christian faith comes and grows through participation in "a particular kind of fellowship," and to encourage parents to strive to transform their family life into a redemptive fellowship of "affection, worship, and work."

The difficulty of this task has been admitted; but no matter how far short of the goal we may fall, the direction of the effort is of primary importance.

Parents with the goal of a Christian family fellowship in mind will the more quickly recognize the inevitable lapses and failures. They will the more readily seek and give forgiveness for intentional and unintentional hurts. They will more quickly and earnestly strive to re-establish loving relationships after disruptive quarrels and misunderstandings.

The child's humpty-dumpty toy, that comic little figure which, as soon and as often as it is knocked down, springs back to an upright position, can be for us an encouraging reminder of our role as parents. Anger, fatigue, illness, selfishness, insensitivity, jealousy, anxiety, self-pity, and countless other human sins and weaknesses are constantly assaulting the fellowship we are striving to establish. The strains and stresses of "life with family" can easily throw us off balance again and again; but the recognized goal of loving family relationships centered in faith in God and in his power at work within us can provide the powerful force that pulls us back each time to our true selves.

PART II

The Bible and Your Child

The greatest Gospel your child will ever know is not the Gospel According to Matthew or Mark, or Luke, or John but the Gospel According to Father and Mother.

Part of the service of baptism of children used by Dr. George Clark Vincent, for many years pastor of the Union Congregational Church, Upper Montclair, New Jersey

CHAPTER 10

According to Father and Mother

From the consideration of the Church and the family as redemptive fellowships, we turn now to the discussion of "the Gospel According to Father and Mother."

The responsibility of the parent in the Christian education of the children has already been stressed. This includes the interpretation of "the Gospel," the Christian faith by which the family seeks to live. The fact that you may feel yourself to be unqualified or unprepared for this task does not release you from its urgency. You are already interpreting some gospel to your child by the way you live, by every word you say, by every act you do. As Christian parents you have a responsibility to know your own faith and to be consistent in your presentation of it.

This gospel according to Father and Mother (whether Christian or secular) will be unquestioningly accepted by the children in their early years. In course of time, they will be exposed to many different points of view regarding the Christian faith. Even in the church school children frequently encounter conflicting beliefs.

"Mom, our teacher said something in church school today that I don't believe you and Dad would agree with," said an eleven-year-old boy at the dinner table one Sunday. And so began a long discussion of some of the basic beliefs of the family's religion.

Not all children bring their confusions and perplexities out into the open. Nor are all children clear enough in their own minds as to their parents' beliefs to raise such questions.

Confusion often arises from conversations with friends of other church affiliations or of different faiths, but in the early years the views of the parents will usually prevail over those of other people.

In the adolescent years, however, this may not be true. In the struggle for selfhood, the need for independence may bring with it a denial of the parents' ways of thinking and doing, a rejection of the parents' gospel.

Outside the home, the young person's faith may be rudely challenged. Few people go through college without having to give a reason for the faith that is in them, without coming into conflict with agnostic and atheistic philosophies.

The chance of a child's faith standing firm through adolescence seems to be greater if all through his developing years he has been encouraged to search for honest answers to his thoughtful questions; if his opinions have been respected, and he has learned to respect the differing opinions of others; if he has been helped to sense the limitations of human knowledge, and if his imagination has been stirred by the deep mysteries that challenge the minds and hearts of men.

MAKE THE BIBLE RELEVANT

In the effort to help a child enter understandingly into his Christian heritage, no parent can afford to ignore the Bible. In Christian fellowship, either Church or family, the Bible rightfully holds a unique place. Here is the record of God's action in history; the long years of preparation, culminating in his revelation of himself in Jesus Christ, and the account of the beginnings of the Christian Church. Here is the foundation for the family's faith.

The following chapters are an attempt to help parents as they explore the Bible with the children and seek to make it relevant to family living today.

The author is well aware of the difficulty of the task. The Bible is many things to many people. Whole libraries have been written about it. In the brief space of the present book the most that can be hoped for is to suggest some directions for thinking and exploring. This book makes no claim to being a theological treatise, although it necessarily touches on theological questions. Readers may find here opinions and interpretations unacceptable to them. To the writer this seems comparatively unimportant. We are dealing with an area where many different opinions are inevitable, and the interpretation suggested is only one possibility.

The important thing is that parents should recognize the need for honest answers to the children's honest questions. Catechetical answers are not good enough; they tend to dull the child's curiosity and discourage his efforts at thinking for himself.

The writer shares with many parents today a concern that boys and girls should be helped to enter more fully into their Christian heritage in the Bible, to develop a surer faith in God, as revealed in Jesus; that they should be encouraged in the struggle to make the faith their own by fearless thinking, facing doubts courageously; that they should never lose a sense of awe at the mystery underlying life; that they should be led to repeated commitments to the Christian way of life.

It is the writer's hope that differences in points of view will serve only to stimulate further prayerful study; and that parents may find their own understanding and appreciation of the Bible deepened as they seek to explore it with their children.

CHAPTER 11

The Need for Self-Education

"Thy word is a lamp to my feet and a light to my path." So sang the psalmist. (Psalms 119:105) But the Bible cannot be a light to our daily living if it remains a closed book gathering dust on a bookshelf.

Many parents today, unfortunately, are ignorant of the Bible and are at a loss to know how to avail themselves of its resources. It needs to be said at the outset that the challenge of finding in the Bible spiritual resources and applying them to family living cannot be met by a casual, halfhearted attempt. Parents can succeed in this effort only if they are sufficiently concerned to pay the price required. A continuous process of self-education demanding time, thought, and persistence is part of the price.

Several difficulties face the beginning student of the Bible. The sheer mass of material is formidable. Here in this one book are in reality sixty-six books, comprising practically all forms of literature: folklore, history, drama, biography, poetry, fiction, letters, sermons, philosophy. The bulk of this collection of writings is enough to dismay busy parents. How much more must it dismay children when they first reach out tentative hands for this strange and bewildering book!

The format in which the Bible is usually printed is monotonous and uninteresting, with its closely spaced, fine-printed pages, and its artificial divisions into chapters and verses. This is not easy reading for people today, accustomed as we are to taking our reading in predigested, capsule doses.

A still more serious difficulty lies in the need for background information. These sixty-six books were written or compiled over a period of more than a thousand years. Each one was produced for a particular purpose, at a particular time in history. Most of them are far from being self-explanatory.

For these difficulties, however, help is readily available to the earnest student. As far as the mass of material is concerned, parents need to keep in mind their purpose—the discovery of spiritual resources for daily living. In the light of this purpose, even a casual turning of the pages of the Bible will soon reveal that not all of its many pages are of equal interest and value. In the first dozen chapters, for instance, are two, Genesis 5 and 10, consisting almost entirely of "the generations of Adam" and "the generations of Noah." No one today need be deeply concerned with these long lists of names.

Or turn a little farther on to the book of Leviticus. Here you will find page after page, chapter after chapter, of the laws of the early Hebrews. These are interesting in their revelation of how laws, believed by the Hebrews to have been given by God, controlled all the details of their daily lives. These pages can be read for their historic interest, but it is not to be expected that in them much will be found to sustain our spiritual life today.

In the study of the Bible much can be passed over quickly; but much will be found to be kept in the heart and pondered long and deeply. The pearls of Bible wisdom and inspiration, however, cannot be discovered unless the search for them is undertaken.

MODERN TRANSLATIONS AND COMMENTARIES

The difficulty of format and arrangement has been partially overcome in modern translations and in some printings of the Bible in shortened form.[1] In some of these, paragraphs have replaced verse-chapter arrangements, quotation marks have been inserted, and poetry has been indicated by its lines.

Access to several modern translations of the Bible will prove interesting and valuable. Many homes now have copies of *The Holy Bible: Revised Standard Version* (New York: Thomas Nelson & Sons, 1952). This is a scholarly translation of early manuscripts. It clarifies many of the obscure passages in the King James Version; it preserves the true meaning by substituting modern words for old words of which the original meaning has changed.

Several other translations are well worth studying, particularly *The New Testament in Modern English,* translated by J. B. Phillips (New York: The Macmillan Company, 1963); *The New English Bible* (England: Oxford University Press, 1961); and *The Bible: A New Translation,* James Moffatt (New York: Harper & Brothers, 1922).

The need for background information can be overcome if there is a good Bible commentary available. This can give insight into the various books, and the purposes for which they were written, as well as verse-by-verse comment and interpretation. *The Interpreter's Bible* (twelve volumes) published by Abingdon Press, Nashville, Tennessee, can be of invaluable help. A set may be available in church or public library.

Vast light has been shed on the meaning and background of the Bible text in recent years. The discovery of the Dead Sea Scrolls and other early manuscripts, and the exciting archeological expeditions unearthing ancient cities are building up new knowledge and new understandings. Again, see the Bibliography for suggested volumes.

[1] See Bibliography: "Bibles and Books about the Bible."

For those parents truly desirous of embarking on a serious study of their Biblical heritage, a number of possible plans are given below.

Some parents may like to begin their study by reading *The Story of the Bible* by Walter Russell Bowie (Nashville: Abingdon Press, 1934). This book includes much helpful interpretation embodying the results of modern Biblical scholarship. It follows the Bible text accurately and is reverently and beautifully written. It would provide a good general background for further study.

A somewhat different approach would be a study of Harry Emerson Fosdick's *A Guide to Understanding the Bible* (New York: Harper & Brothers, 1938; Torchlight edition, 1956). In this volume, Dr. Fosdick deals with several important ideas: the ideas of God, of man, of right and wrong, of suffering, of fellowship with God, of immortality. In each instance he begins with the earliest writings and shows how the primitive idea, in the course of centuries, changed and developed, concluding with the fruition of the idea in the teaching of Jesus. It is impossible to read this book intelligently without constant reference to the Bible itself; but studied in this way, unhurriedly, it provides the reader with deep understandings and rare insights.

Some parents may like to begin their study of the Bible by searching out and reading half-remembered stories and passages, consulting *The Interpreter's Bible* or other commentary for additional enlightenment as to their meaning and significance. From this beginning they may go on to less familiar material. Access to a concordance would be necessary for this plan.[2]

Another plan which may prove interesting is to study the books of the Bible in the chronological order in which they were written, rather than following the order of arrangement in the Bible.[3]

[2] See Appendix II: "A Partial Concordance of Bible Material."
[3] See Appendix I.

Some parents may prefer to begin their study of the New Testament leaving the Old Testament till later. Here, too, the chronological approach may be of interest.

Parents may find it helpful to base their own Bible study on the passages used as a basis for the children's church school curriculum. Many church schools send home magazines or quarterlies containing this information.

So much for the parents' efforts to overcome their Biblical illiteracy through self-directed study at home. Before concluding this section on the parents' need for greater Biblical knowledge, mention must be made of several avenues of help open to concerned parents.

It is probably unnecessary to point out that participation in the Sunday morning services of worship exposes parents to the use of the Bible in worship and to interpretation of texts from the pulpit. This is a source of information and understanding of which every parent should take full advantage.

Many churches provide an adult Bible class and make available to their members commentaries, concordances, and other reference books. Where this is not done every Sunday, a series of meetings for this purpose is often held several times a year.

In many places a Community Council of Churches sponsors a school of religion, a co-operative undertaking of particular value to members of small churches with limited leadership. These schools usually offer a series of six meetings, one night a week, once or twice a year, and almost invariably include one Bible study course.

During the last few years the producers of moving pictures have drawn upon the Bible for some of their most spectacular productions. While these need to be viewed critically (for sometimes accuracy is sacrificed for dramatic effect) it is still true that they picture vividly and unforgettably the Bible stories and present a wealth of detail regarding life in those long-ago centuries. Reading the Bible material upon which the pictures are based will be a protection against the inevitable distortion of some of the story elements.

Parents may study the Bible for a number of different reasons, but surely the best of reasons is the purpose to find God and be found of him. Dr. Buttrick reminds us that

> the Bible, despite frequent avowals, is not in original instance a book of "man's quest for God." Initially, in prime purpose it is intent to show that no quest on man's part is possible except under God's prompting. Our search for him is quickened by his prior finding of us. . . . It is not an earthbound book either of literature or science, history or human quest: its sole and all-comprehending purpose is to tell of the invasion of earth by heaven's succor and demand. The reader is not required in any dark coercion to believe this claim "sight unseen," but he should understand the claim. Moreover, it is fair to ask that he expose himself to it. So the study of the Bible requires him to say, whether neophyte or theologian, "Generations of people have said that God has found them through this Book. I will be neither servile nor embattled, but will give the Book its chance with me." A man must approach the study of the Bible with the right presuppositions.[4]

[4] From *The Interpreter's Bible,* Vol. 1, p. 166. Copyright 1952 by Pierce and Smith (Abingdon Press).

CHAPTER 12

Catching Your Child's Interest

It is a strange fact that even parents who are themselves quite ignorant of the Bible still want their children to know it. Among the most persistent criticisms leveled against the modern church school is that "it doesn't teach enough Bible."

Thoughtful parents these days realize uneasily that even though their children are enrolled in an excellent church school where many significant things are happening, their knowledge of the Bible is appallingly limited—and likely to remain so.

Some parents facing this realization are inclined to blame the church school. "What's the matter?" they ask. "Why aren't they teaching the Bible any more? What's happened to all the Bible stories I learned when I was a youngster?"

Actually many church schools today are doing a highly creditable job against almost insuperable obstacles. Few of the critics face squarely the inevitable limitation in the amount of Bible knowledge even the best church school can hope to impart.

Consider for a moment the time element. It has been estimated that a single reading of the entire Bible, with no allowance for re-reading, or discussion, or using a commentary, or memorizing—just a single reading straight through would take an average adult reader approximately sixty hours. A junior boy or girl would undoubtedly take much longer, perhaps 125 hours. This is almost two and a half times the total amount of time the usual child spends in church school *in an entire year,* even if he is present every single Sunday, including July and August. If a period of forty minutes each Sunday is devoted to Bible study, the total amount of time in a year for this purpose would be about thirty-five hours. When from this maximum possible time are deducted the special service days, and the time lost by absences because of illness, or family weekend trips, or parental indifference, the number of hours available for Bible study in the church school is seen to be startlingly inadequate.

Teachers recognize an additional difficulty in that even these scanty hours are broken up into small bits, separated by intervals of a week or more, making steady, continuous progress extremely difficult. Opposition to "homework" in church school seems to be fairly universal, adding still another obstacle.

Those parents, therefore, who are depending on the church school to bear the total responsibility for providing their children with any reasonable degree of Biblical literacy are doomed to disappointment. It is unrealistic to expect it.

WHAT IS YOUR PURPOSE?

Many of those who are declaring, "I want my child to know the Bible," are sometimes quite taken aback if confronted with the simple question, "Why?" The answer is not so simple as might appear at first glance. In striving to reply honestly, some parents have said the following:

"I want my child to know the Bible so that he may recognize and understand the innumerable references and illustrations drawn from it that are scattered through the literature of all ages. It is a part of his literary heritage."

"It seems to me it's important for my daughter to know the Bible as a source book of strength and comfort in her everyday experiences."

"A study of the Bible has given many people a strong Christian faith. These times in which we live cry out for such a faith."

"I want my children to know the Bible because generations have proved its value as an ennobling and uplifting force in human life."

"The New Testament seems much more important to me than the Old. I want my family to be confronted by Jesus Christ. I want them to be won to a growing commitment to Jesus and the Christian way of living."

Even a casual reading of these comments makes it obvious that when parents say "I want my child to know the Bible," they mean something other than mere familiarity with the material contained in these sixty-six books. Superficial knowledge is not enough.

When I was a young parent I lived next door to a man who was a delightful neighbor, a warmhearted, grandfatherly person who was adored by the children, and of whom I grew to be very fond. We had not lived side by side long, however, before we each discovered something rather startling about the other. He discovered that I was deeply involved in Christian education; I found out that he was a freethinker whose major concern was to "debunk" the Bible!

This man had studied the Bible exhaustively, but only for the purpose of finding and exposing its many contradictions and inconsistencies. *He knew his Bible.* He could quote chapter and verse with truly amazing facility. And yet his knowledge was superficial. Never once had he seen the Bible as a record of God's continuous endeavor to break through the barriers of man's ignorance, superstition, willfulness, and indifference to reveal himself; or as a record of struggling, bewildered, often mistaken people seeking to discover the meaning of existence. This man knew only the shell of the Bible; its deepest meaning he never discovered.

And yet to him and others like him we today owe a debt of gratitude. At least partly because of their activities, we have been freed from the too literalistic interpretation of the Bible

text that was for many years a stumbling block to true understanding. Today we are free to know and love the Bible without doing violence to our intelligence. We know that the Bible
is a book of religion; we do not expect it to be a scientific
textbook. We can open our hearts and minds freely to the
religious truth so poetically expressed: "In the beginning God
created," and "the Spirit of God was moving over the face of
the waters." (Genesis 1:1, 2)

In spite of the removal of some difficulties and a greater
opportunity for an intelligent appreciation of our Biblical
heritage, the sad fact is that most adult Christians and nearly
all children and young people today are woefully ignorant
about it.

> . . . it is precarious to risk a biblical allusion, even in so-called
> "educated" circles, if one is at all anxious to be understood. The
> great majority of the young of today have not been taught the
> Bible at their mothers' knee, nor heard it read aloud at family
> prayers or in church; they know as little about it as they do about
> Homer or Vergil. This is a disturbing thought, for the com-
> bined heritages of classical and biblical antiquity have hitherto
> given our western civilization whatever ideal meaning and pur-
> pose it has ever had.[1]

If this regrettable situation is to be remedied in the fore-
seeable future, it is today's parents who must bring about the
change. For our children we want more than superficial
knowledge of the Bible. We want a growing familiarity with
its content, accompanied by increased understanding, and by
a constantly deepening appreciation of the Bible as containing
the revelation of God. We want this increasing knowledge,
understanding, and appreciation to *make a difference* in the
children's lives as they come to "know the Bible" in the only
way it can be truly known—by testing its teachings in the
present workaday world of human living-together.

[1] Basil Willey in *The Bible Today* (New York: Harper & Brothers, in
co-operation with *The Times,* London, 1955), pp. 66–67.

THE DIFFICULTIES FOR CHILDREN

The difficulties in the study of the Bible noted in the previous chapter are even greater for children. Pick up at random any one of the books that the children evidently enjoy. Notice its convenient size; leaf through the pages. Observe the large print, the wide margins, the small amount of printed matter on each page, the colorful illustrations. Now pick up the Bible. The contrast is immediately obvious. No child would ever be spontaneously attracted to the Bible in its usual format, nor would he be likely of his own accord to try to dig out from its pages the parts that can have value and meaning for him.

Many attempts have been made over the years to overcome the forbidding format of the Bible. Perhaps the earliest attempt to increase its attractiveness was to furnish it with illustrations. Unfortunately early illustrators selected as themes for their pictures the most lurid and dramatic episodes. They portrayed frightful devils with horns and tails. They delighted in scenes of violence and bloodshed. They vividly depicted bodies writhing in hell in the torment of perpetual flames.

In my childhood the family observance of Sunday followed the social pattern of fairly rigid restrictions on children's activities. The use of all such toys as bicycles, tricycles, and skates was strictly forbidden. Reading, with some limitations, was permitted. Three fairly large, red-bound volumes, standing on a low shelf of the bookcase were looked upon with favor. These were books of page-size black-and-white illustrations of the Bible, with brief sections of Scripture under each picture. I have a distinct recollection, dating back to the days before I could read, of sitting on the bottom step of the stairs beside my older sister, poring over these pictures with wide and wondering eyes.

Only one picture has remained in my memory through the years, but that one is a vivid memory: a raging, swirling flood, an uprooted tree, one or two frightened animals swimming desperately, the only land visible a single point of rock projecting perhaps two feet above the water, and clinging to the rock with one hand a woman, her other hand upraised and holding above the flood a tiny baby. So vivid was the picture that every time I looked at it I expected to see the woman's hand slip off the rock and to see both mother and baby disappear beneath the angry waters. Inseparably connected with my horror at that picture was the knowledge that *God had sent the flood*.

Many attempts at illustrating the Bible have probably done more harm than good. Recent years have seen the eruption into print of a number of "Bible comics." (Than which no less appropriate title could possibly have been found!) Producers and buyers of these strip pictures justify them on the basis that here is an easy, painless way for the children to become familiar with the Bible stories. But what happens to the children's understanding of the Bible as they pore over these cheap and lurid story sheets? Perhaps the acquaintance with a few Bible characters and incidents thus portrayed is a high price to pay for the damage done to a child's sense of the uniqueness, the "specialness" of the Bible.

Fortunately, this is only one side to the picture. Over the years a good many people have recognized the need to present Bible material to children in a less forbidding and more attractive format. The result is that today a number of books are available that are intended to introduce children to the Bible and provide background knowledge of life and customs in Bible times. The best of these books are excellent, beautiful examples of the best in children's literature. Parents need, however, to choose from the books offered with discrimination and careful judgment.[2]

All of these picture-story books, however, are not an end in themselves. They are preliminaries to the child's use of the Bible itself. Sooner or later the child will hold in his hands

[2] A list of books recommended because of their wise selection of material, their sound scholarship, and artistic format is given in the Bibliography.

his very own "real" Bible, and will be ready to begin his lifetime study of God's Word.

A number of church schools present each boy and girl with a Bible, often at the end of the third grade. Most children look forward to this gift and reach out eager hands for it. It is sad that so frequently there follows a sense of disappointment, for the children's first ventures in reading their own Bibles may prove to be completely frustrating.

Fortunate is the child who finds a parent ready to stand by and help with knowledge and insight, a parent who knows where to find familiar passages, a parent who can clear away misunderstandings and let the true message of the Bible speak to a child's soul. A few minutes spent with the child, sharing his pleasure in his own Bible, guiding him in his first explorations, and promising him further help as needed will be richly repaid.

If the Bible provided does not have a concordance, parents may find it difficult to locate on demand any particular story or passage.[3]

Recognizing the difficulties children face in finding familiar passages, I find it hard to understand why many people object to marking the Bible. It seems to me if this is done carefully and reverently it can be a great help to a child. Various methods can be used. Of course, the simplest way is to draw a line in the margin beside the familiar verses. A special, colored pencil could be used for this, and at first the marking should be done only under supervision. Another method is to use narrow strips of gummed tape (about ⅛-inch wide); silver is attractive. It may be that memorized passages may have some special marking of their own—a different color perhaps. This might add incentive to memory work. Ribbon bookmarks to put in special places are also a help.

Parents will want to provide opportunities for the child to read from his own Bible at family-together times. The reading of selected passages for family memorization (see Chapter

[3] See Appendix II: "A Partial Concordance of Bible Material." See also Chapter 14: "The Bible for Various Ages."

15) may well be the child's responsibility. One thing is certain, the child will need a great deal of help and encouragement over a considerable period of time if the Bible is ever to speak to him, personally and individually, in a way that he can comprehend.

In handling the Bible with boys and girls, it helps to recognize and admit that the Bible is not primarily a book written for children. It is obviously a book meant for adults. It is not the format alone that is forbidding; the content also presents its own difficulties. No one can read far in its pages without coming upon abstruse and involved passages, the meaning of which is uncertain even to learned scholars who have spent years in the study of the Bible. The next chapters will endeavor to give some help in understanding and interpreting some few difficulties.

The fact, however, that the Bible is an adult book may well be turned to good account in challenging the child's interest. "Most of the books you read," a parent may say, "you read once or twice or perhaps several times, but then you outgrow them and they don't interest you any more. But the Bible is one book that you'll come back to over and over again. Of course right now, there are only a few parts of it here and there that you can understand and enjoy. But as you grow older, you'll find more and more in it to interest you. This is one book you'll never outgrow."

It is encouraging, moreover, to realize that children catch the enthusiasms of their parents. Boys and girls growing up in a home where good music is enjoyed quite naturally develop an interest in good music. A boy whose father likes to work with tools is eager to share that grown-up interest. Small boys playing doctor, or traffic cop, or bus driver, small girls playing mother, or nurse, or teacher, or ballet dancer, are all spontaneously trying to enter into and understand adult occupations and enthusiasms.

The conclusion is obvious. You want your children to be interested in the Bible. The sure-fire method for developing that interest is plain: *let them know that you are genuinely interested in it yourself.* Let them see you reading it. Let them know when you attend an adult Bible class. Talk about the Bible passages used in the church service. Watch for comments from the children about Bible material used in church school; be ready to show them where in the Bible are to be found the verses they mention. Store up in your memory certain Bible verses that have deep meaning for you and share them with the family at appropriate moments. Be alert to references to the Bible in modern literature, of which there are many, and for related magazine articles and news items. Even a small child's imagination can be caught by the unearthing of buried cities.

You want your child to know the Bible? Nothing is so contagious as enthusiastic interest.

CHAPTER 13

Emphasis on the New Testament

We may heartily agree with the writer of 2 Timothy that

> All scripture is inspired by God and profitable for teaching, for reproof, for correction, and for training in righteousness. . . . (2 Timothy 3:16)

But we are still faced with difficulty as we seek to use Scripture for training our children "in righteousness." The problem is to discover the particular Scripture that is most appealing, and then to use it effectively so that it makes the highest possible contribution to the child's developing religious life.

It is perhaps fortunate that a child's first ventures into the Bible's content must necessarily be guided and directed. For in that very circumstance may lie his protection from many disturbing and puzzling passages for which he is not yet ready. The parent cannot read long in the Bible without stumbling on unsavory bits that are surely not desirable for children's reading. No tabloid is more outspoken on sex than certain passages in the Bible. No "comic" book outdoes it in vivid portrayal of violence and bloodshed.

THE SHOCKING STORIES

Even its most familiar and best-loved stories contain many disturbing and sometimes shocking episodes. Consider the following:

Here is a story of a man who kills his brother because of jealousy. Genesis 4:3–16.

Here is a story of a mother conspiring with her younger son to defraud his elder brother of his rightful inheritance, and deceiving her blind husband as part of the scheme. Genesis 27:1–45.

Here is a tale of a group of brothers who planned to kill their younger brother, but instead sold him into slavery; and who took his robe, dipped it in the blood of an animal, and brought it to their father, keeping their ugly secret for many years. Genesis 37:12–36.

Here is one of a woman who, for a quantity of silver pieces, used her allurement to find out the secret of her lover's strength, and handed him over to his enemies for torture and eventual death. Judges 16.

Here is one of a woman who offered her tent as a hiding place to a soldier fleeing for his life, telling him to "have no fear"; and who, when he slept, took a tent peg and a hammer, and "drove the peg into his temple, till it went down into the ground." Judges 4:17–22.

Here is one of a king who, looking from his housetop, saw a beautiful woman bathing, sent to have her brought to him, and subsequently plotted successfully to have her husband killed so she could be his wife. "But the thing that David had done displeased the Lord." 2 Samuel 11.

This literature is strong meat—not to be thought of as a collection of nursery tales or bedtime stories! Surely great and important teachings are to be derived from these tales, but at what age are our children ready to profit from such mental diet? A certain degree of maturity is obviously desirable and some sense of the historic development of civilization before boys and girls are ready to set these stories into an intelligent framework and get from them the values that are imbedded in them.

The parent's purpose in the use of Bible material has been thoughtfully stated as follows:

"to make available for our children *the accumulated treasures of Christian life and thought in such a way that God in Christ may carry on His redemptive work in each human soul and in the common life of man.*"[1]

Such a purpose throws the emphasis of our teaching where it rightly belongs—on the New Testament. It is the *Christian* way of life, it is the *Christian* faith with which we are concerned.

This does not mean that we leave out the Old Testament— far from it. But it does mean that Old Testament material is considered and evaluated in the light of the New.

An interesting example of this way of judging Old Testament stories is revealed in the following true incident.

A group of nine-year-olds were studying about Moses. The story had been shortened and much of the Bible narrative had been omitted. One morning, just as the group was settling down for the session, Arnold burst into the room. "You know, Miss Johnson," he began, even before he got his coat off, "you didn't tell us all of the story. You left out some of the most interesting part." And in a torrent of words, Arnold proceeded to fill in the gaps. "And when Moses led the Hebrews out of Egypt," he declared finally, "they took a lot of the cattle of the Egyptians with them. And that was all right because Moses knew they would need food and things when they got over into the wilderness." He paused for breath and the leader stalled for time to think.

"Arnold has told us some more of the story," she said. "And he is right in what he has told. When you read the story in the Bible, you'll find all this and more too." By this time she was ready to face some of the questions raised. "I was interested," she went on, "in what Arnold said about the Hebrews taking the cattle of the Egyptians. Arnold says he thinks that was perfectly all right. Let's talk about it." Her tone was noncommittal, expressing neither approval nor disagreement.

"Oh, sure," said one boy, easily. "That was all right. Why look how Pharaoh had been treating the Hebrews!"

"Yes," broke in another. "Look at how he'd made slaves of them. And put men with whips to watch them."

[1] Dora F. Chaplin, *Children and Religion* (New York: Charles Scribner's Sons, 1946), p. 220.

"And made them make bricks without giving them straw," added a third.

The leader nodded. "Yes, that's all true," she said. "He had treated them shamefully."

"And Moses knew," broke in Arnold, "that when he got the people into the wilderness they'd starve to death if they did not take food with them." The leader nodded. The group seemed in perfect agreement.

Suddenly Daniel stood up. "Miss Johnson," he said, slowly and hesitantly, "you know, I've been thinking—I don't believe Jesus would have said that was the right thing to do."

The leader took a moment to be sure her voice was still non-committal. "Don't you, Daniel?" she asked then. "Why not?"

The boy just looked at her, frowning. "I don't know exactly," he said. "But I just don't think he would."

The leader turned to the group. "Daniel says," she repeated quietly, "that he does not think that Jesus would have said that was the right thing to do. How about it?" There followed a moment of deep and thoughtful silence. The leader waited.

"I guess he's right," admitted a boy, reluctantly. "You know Jesus said it didn't matter what anyone did to you, you had to do the right thing anyhow."

"Return good for evil," said another suddenly.

"It really was stealing," admitted a third.

"And Jesus said, 'Do good to those who hate you,'" volunteered another. There was no dissenting voice.[2]

Daniel was judging Old Testament stories in the light of his knowledge of Jesus. In following such a procedure, we have ample justification in Jesus' own treatment of Scripture. He was thoroughly familiar with the sacred literature of his people. The Gospel stories are generously sprinkled with his references to the scrolls. But over and over again Jesus says, "You have heard—*but I say*—" (Matthew 5:21, 27, 33, 38, 43) and in each instance these words are followed by a higher and more profound moral demand. In each instance Jesus *goes beyond* the Old Testament moral standards.

In selecting Bible material for use with children parents may well be governed by the following rule: at first, use

[2] From *Their Rightful Heritage*, by Florence M. Taylor. Copyright, 1942, Florence M. Taylor. The Pilgrim Press. Used by permission.

only those passages and stories which illuminate the New Testament faith, or at least do not contradict any of its basic teachings. As the children grow older and begin to catch some sense of history, the stories containing unchristian ideas and points of view can be set in proper perspective, and can be used to point up ever more clearly the supreme revelation of God in Jesus.

A WORD OF CAUTION

A caution about how to use the Bible stories and passages may be in order. Only as their experiences with the Bible are happy will children come to love it. Parents must resist the temptation to quote the Bible at children in those distressing times when the loving fellowship of the home has been temporarily disrupted by flaring tempers or sour dispositions. It is true that the Bible teachings are definitely relevant to such situations; it is also true that implied condemnation of actions in a Bible quotation will probably do little to help at the particular moment. These are times for parents *to quote the Bible to themselves,* not to the children; to hold fast to "Love is patient and kind—is not irritable or resentful —endures all things" (1 Corinthians 13:4–7); "A soft answer turns away wrath, but a harsh word stirs up anger." (Proverbs 15:1)

In attempting to choose Bible material for various ages, it needs to be recognized that no selection could possibly fit all situations. Children any given chronological age range in mental age over a span of several years. No parent needs to be reminded that children differ widely in their interests and abilities.

The proper time to introduce a particular Bible story or passage depends on many things. For instance, Dorothy and Peter (see page 30) because of their own experience would probably be ready to listen with understanding and appreciation to the story of Zacchaeus—a man who "needed an awful lot of loving" and whose need was met by Jesus. Ordinarily that particular story would be more meaningful to children a little older.

No matter how carefully a parent selects Bible material the children are quite apt to come in contact at any time with stories which parents would have preferred to postpone. Obviously these have to be handled if and when they are heard.

The next chapter will recommend some Bible material for various ages, with some reasons for including or excluding particular passages at particular times. Later chapters will deal with some major difficulties in Bible content and will seek to give helpful suggestions for interpretation.

CHAPTER 14

The Bible for Various Ages

The suggestions given in this chapter for Bible material most apt to be of value and interest to various ages are not meant to be rigidly applied. Parents in the intimacy of family life will know better than anyone else the range and depth of their children's understandings. These few chosen stories and passages, however, may serve as a beginning for family exploration of the Bible.

Bearing in mind points already presented in previous chapters, it would seem that certain basic principles are relevant to the selection and use of any Bible material at any time.

Selections will be used purposefully: in order to make available "the accumulated treasures of Christian life in such a way that God in Christ may carry on his redemptive work in each human soul and in the common life of man."

Major emphasis for this purpose will be placed upon the New Testament, especially on the life and teachings of Jesus. Old Testament materials will be read and evaluated in the light of the New. (See Chapter 13)

Stories or passages in which pre-Christian ideas of God appear will be carefully explained and interpreted in order not to do violence to a child's developing relationship to God "the Father of our Lord, Jesus Christ." (See further discussion of this in Chapter 16.)

Differences of belief, when encountered, will be met frankly and matter-of-factly, with care being exercised to respect any honestly held point of view. Wherever it is possible, it will be helpful to find beneath the difference any possible agreement. (For example: "Roman Catholics believe . . . and Protestants believe . . . but we all are followers of Jesus.")

FOR CHILDREN UNDER SIX

Parents seeking Bible stories or passages within the understanding of children under six may well become discouraged at the paucity of appropriate material. Probably not more than six or eight suitable Bible stories will be found, and even these must be reduced to very simple terms.

It must be recognized that these small children are "receiving the Gospel" not so much through spoken words as through the total loving, supporting environment of the home.

The Nativity stories in very simple form will of course be part of the Christmas observance. (See *The First Christmas* by Phoebe Anderson, listed in Bibliography I.)

Some comments about the boy Jesus, probably in connection with pictures, will be interesting. Perhaps the small picture book *When Jesus Was a Boy* (see Bibliography I) may be enjoyed. Jesus' trip to Jerusalem when he was twelve may be described, again with pictures of things he may have seen along the way. (Omit the incident of his lingering behind in the Temple—Luke 2:41–52.)

Similar comments, or simple story-talks, may be made about pictures of Jesus with the children, with his fisherman friends, with people on the hillside, or sitting in a boat talking to the people along the shore.

From the Old Testament the choice is even more limited. It may be that a few pictures of shepherd life may lead to

the story of "Isaac of the Tents" (see Bibliography I) and
perhaps to a very much simplified story of "The Tent Church."
(Exodus 35:4–29)

A Caution: several stories sometimes used with this age
group would seem to be better a few years later. One is the
story of Creation (Genesis 1), which is better used when it
can be interpreted as one of the "how-stories" of the early
Hebrews. (See below under "For Children Nine to Twelve.")
Another is the story of Noah's Ark (Genesis 6, 7, 8). While
the two-by-two procession of animals may seem at first a
fascinating tale for the youngsters, the *reason* for the Ark,
God's presumed anger at men, and the imminent destructive
flood are completely unsuitable for small tots.

Another story, the use of which at this age would seem to
be ill-advised, is the story of the baby Moses. Again, the
center of the story, the baby hidden in the basket, has a
certain appeal, but without some background knowledge of
the reason for hiding the baby, and some indication of Moses' place in the history of his people, the baby incident is
innocuous. It is much better handled later as part of the
whole story of Moses. (Exodus 2:1–10)

Information about the Bible. During these early years, the
small child is already receiving his first impressions of the
Bible. He learns that it is a very special book that the grown-
ups love, that the minister reads from it in church; that
mother and father often read it at home (or never read it at
home?); that it has stories in it about Jesus—the lovely
Christmas stories and others.

Memorization. Although no emphasis will be put on memorizing during these years, if as part of a family group the
small children are exposed to Bible verses meaningfully used,
they will soon begin to learn them by heart. "Wonder verses"
and "thankful verses" may soon in this way become part of
a child's language of worship.

One four-year-old learned the following prayer verses from
the Bible and used them as her special grace:

Thou art the God who doest wonders.
PSALMS 77:14, KJ

Many, O Lord my God, are thy wonderful works
which thou has done.
PSALMS 40:5, KJ

Thou hast put gladness in my heart.
PSALMS 4:7, KJ

In thy presence is fulness of joy.
PSALMS 16:11, KJ

FOR CHILDREN SIX TO EIGHT

The six-to-eight years of childhood are a time of constantly widening horizons. Now a wealth of Bible stories can be enjoyed.

In the New Testament the following incidents in Jesus' life told in simple words, but following the Bible narrative closely, should become familiar: the Nativity stories (Luke 2:1–20; Matthew 2:1–12); the presentation in the temple (Luke 2:22–24); the flight into Egypt (Matthew 2:13–15); the return to Nazareth (Matthew 2:19–23); the trip to Jerusalem (Luke 2:41–52); Jesus choosing his helpers (Mark 1:16–20; 2:13–14; 3:13–19; John 1:43–47); Jesus' own use of prayer (Mark 1:35–38); Jesus teaching from a boat (Luke 5:1–3); and on the mountain (Matthew 5, 6 and 7, selected verses); healing the man let down through the roof (Mark 2:1–12); Jesus and Zacchaeus (Luke 19:1–8).

Some of Jesus' teachings are good material for this age group; the Two Commandments (Matthew 22:35–40), the Good Samaritan (Luke 10:25–37), the Lost Sheep (Matthew 18:12–14).

From the Old Testament come a number of stories suitable for this age: Abraham giving Lot first choice (Genesis 13:2 –12); Isaac and the Wells (Genesis 26:18–22); Jacob's dream, omitting the details of the reason for his flight from home (Genesis 28:10–19); Naaman's little maid (2 Kings 5:1–14); Samuel helping Eli, omitting his hearing God's voice (1 Samuel 1; 2:18–20); stories of David—Saul's musician (1 Samuel 16:14–23), friendship with Jonathan (1 Samuel 18:1–4), kindness to Jonathan's son (2 Samuel 9:1 –13).

Information about the Bible. The six- to eight-year-olds, especially the older children in this group, are beginning to handle the Bible themselves.

By the end of this period they have probably picked up a considerable number of facts about the Bible: they may know that it is really sixty-six books in one; that it is in two parts, the Old Testament and the New; that the New Testament contains the stories of Jesus and his friends; that the Psalms was the hymnbook of the early Hebrews; that the Bible was first written by hand on scrolls, and copied and recopied before men had invented printing; that the Bible was not originally written in English; that today parts of the Bible have been translated and printed in more than 1100 languages and dialects. They may have some rather vague idea that the Bible is "God's Word," and that it is a very special book telling of God and Jesus.

Memorization. Practically all the children at the end of this period will know by heart the Lord's Prayer, the Twenty-third Psalm, and the One Hundredth Psalm. Many will know Jesus' Two Commandments. Most will know, too, a miscellaneous collection of single Bible verses that will probably not be retained unless they are picked up and used frequently at home.

Suggestions for "Memorizing Bible Passages" as a family project are given in Chapter 15. This is a good age with which to begin. Always, however, it needs to be emphasized that the memorizing should be an *enjoyed* experience; that parents should encourage and help, but that it must never become for the children an irksome or unpleasant task.

FOR THE NINE-TO-TWELVES

These years provide the golden opportunity for Bible learning. At this age the boys and girls are shooting out interest sparks in all directions. Now is the time for a connected story of the life of Jesus; for a study of some of his parables and teachings; for coming to grips with the things for which Jesus stood; for seeing him as he was, a revolutionary with a daring dream; and for a growing determination to follow Jesus' way of life.

Now the thrilling and fascinating adventures of Paul may be told, with emphasis not so much on the details of where he went on his various journeys, but rather on the urgency of his faith, as he carried the good news to distant lands.

Now the searching minds of the boys and girls are ready to deal with many Old Testament stories, to recognize the primitive elements, to be caught up by the challenging hero stories. Now they are ready to read the early stories in Genesis, and understand them for what they are—a primitive people's thoughtful answers to the "how's" and "why's" of their existence. Now they need not be puzzled by any seeming conflict between science and religion. They may accept the findings of modern science and still be moved to wonder at the keen religious insight of the early Hebrews, who could look out at the bewildering world and make so daring a claim: "In the beginning, God created!"

The story of the Tower of Babel has a new fascination when it is seen as an answer to the question, "Why are there different languages?" (Genesis 11:1–9) What an interesting early insight that different languages make it difficult for people to work together co-operatively!

The Adam and Eve story takes on deeper significance when it is seen as an attempt to answer how sin and evil began, and to show the nature of sin as disobedience to God, and the result of sin as separation from God. (Genesis 3)

The element of God's anger in the flood story can now be

interpreted as someone's mistaken answer to the "why" of a great inundation that devastated the early world, and the story of Noah and the Ark as an ingenious device to explain the continued existence of life, both of men and of creatures, after the all-covering waters had subsided. (Genesis 6, 7, 8) In discussing this story it may be helpful to call attention to the fact that when floods come in our own country today, no one believes they are caused by the evil-doing of the people living in the area.

This is the age for the stories of Abraham and Isaac and Jacob (Genesis 12–33); of Joseph and his brethren (Genesis 37–50); of Moses (Exodus); of David (1 Samuel 17–2 Samuel) and Solomon (1 Kings 3:1–15; 5–8). Parents will need to do considerable study if they are to guide the boys and girls intelligently. Broadening experience, some beginning sense of history, and maturing insights and understandings are characteristic of this age.

Information about the Bible. The years from nine to twelve usually provide a good deal of knowledge about the Bible itself, and considerable skill in handling it. By the end of this period the children usually know that there are four stories of Jesus, that they are called "gospels," which means "good news," that the Gospel According to Mark was probably the first one to be written; that Matthew and Luke both apparently made use of Mark in writing their stories; and that John was the last to be written.

They may know that the Book of Acts tells about what the disciples did after Jesus died; that much of it is about Paul, who was first a persecutor of the early Christians and later became the first great missionary, spreading the "good news of Jesus" through all the area of the Mediterranean world. The boys and girls may know that "epistle" means "letter" and some selected passages from Paul's letters may begin to be recognized.

Memorization. At this age well-selected passages are memorized with surprising ease and speed. Given encouragement and interest on the part of the parents, and some imagination in providing sufficient motivation on a level that the children understand and accept, there is practically no limit to their powers. See suggestions for "Memorizing Bible Passages," Chapter 15.

Few church schools now take time in class sessions for memorizing the order of the books of the Bible, yet no serious student will deny that such knowledge immensely facilitates the use of the book. If it does not seem important to you, at least you will want to be certain that the children know where the table of contents is located, and that they gain facility in its use.

Those parents who recognize the desirability of helping children memorize the order of the books will probably be surprised at the ease with which it can be accomplished, especially if it is done as a family project with plenty of fun and fellowship as part of the process. Puzzles and games are easily developed that make the learning almost automatic.

Cards of different colors, each color representing a section, may be cut in strips, each strip having printed on it the title of a single book. The colored strips may be placed in separate envelopes, each envelope having the correct order printed on it. As soon as a child is able to arrange the strips in one envelope in correct order without consulting the list, he may be encouraged to try the next envelope. See end of this chapter for "Contents of the Bible" arranged in suitable sections for use in this way.

If the children have among their toys one of the popular electric questioners, an ingenious parent may easily work out a set of cards for use with it, which will test their knowledge of the order of the Bible books. For instance: "What book follows Leviticus?" "In what section is the book of Amos?" etc.

FOR THE TEEN-AGERS

This is the age when all the accumulated bits of Bible knowledge may be gathered up and set in an orderly, connected whole. Either at the end of the previous age group or near the beginning of this, every boy and girl should read a story of the Bible. The one highly recommended is Walter Russell Bowie's *The Story of the Bible* "retold from Genesis to Revelation in the light of present knowledge for both the young and the mature," published by Abingdon Press, 1934.[1]

The interests of teen-agers are so broad that they are ready to be challenged by the social vision of the prophets, and to see in the prophets' messages relevance for our strife-torn world today. They are ready, too, for facing Job's problem and a realistic consideration of suffering and evil.

This is the usual age for a personal commitment to Jesus and his way of life, and for a consequent joining in the fellowship of other declared Christians through membership in the Church.

Information about the Bible. Areas of knowledge to which teen-agers should be exposed and in which they may be expected to find much to interest them include: the romantic story of how the English Bible came into being; accounts of recent archeological discoveries such as the Dead Sea Scrolls; the history of the Christian Church, with particular emphasis on what it means to be a Protestant; the missionary movement over the centuries; the astonishing ecumenical development in recent years.

No young person should grow to maturity in a Christian home without being challenged to apply his Christian philosophy to the choice of his lifework. Obviously not all will or should choose to be ministers, but the meaning of Christian vocation is not limited, and the relevance of Christian belief to every phase of life should be clearly recognized. The parable of the talents has deep meaning here. (Matthew 25:14–30)

If only every young person facing the choice of his life's work could make Kagawa's "Discovery" his own!

[1] The same author has also written *The Story of the Old Testament for Boys and Girls,* and *The Story of the Bible for Youth.* My personal preference is for the one recommended above.

I cannot invent
New things
Like the airships
Which sail
On silver wings;
But today
A wonderful thought
In the dawn was given.

. . . .

And the thought
Was this:
That a secret plan
Is hid in my hand;
That my hand is big,
Big,
Because of this plan.

That God
Who dwells in my hand,
Knows this secret plan
Of the things he will do
for the world
Using my hand.[2]

Georgia Harkness says:

It is not everybody's duty to follow a vocation specifically labeled religious. Nothing much worse could be imagined than for every devout person, regardless of fitness, to decide to be a clergyman! There is perhaps as much need of Christians in politics as in pulpits. But every person ought to choose his vocation in the light of the most inclusive service he can give and in fidelity to his truest ideal of the way of God. . . . Clement of Alexandria, in the second century, described with poetic insight the effect of religious vision upon the tasks of common life:

"Holding festival, then, in our whole life, persuaded that God is altogether on every side present, we cultivate our fields, praising; we sail the sea, hymning; in all the rest of our conversation we conduct ourselves according to rule." (Stromata, VII, 7 in *Anti-Nicene Fathers,* Vol. II, p. 533.)[3]

[2] Toyohiko Kagawa, from *Songs from the Slums* (Nashville: Abingdon-Cokesbury Press, 1935).
[3] Georgia Harkness, *Religious Living* (New York: The Edward W. Hazen Foundation, Inc., distributed by Association Press), pp. 4–5.

Memorization. Probably the interest in memorization will be less in this age group than in the previous one, unless the individual boy or girl has had particularly rewarding experiences in family or church school. What memorizing is done is apt to be on an individual basis, and only because some particular passage has very real and appealing significance; or is to be used in a special service or dramatization.

Many teen-agers are susceptible to suggestions for individual daily devotions, in addition to anything the family does as a whole, and may find helpful some of the ideas in Chapters 8 and 9.

CONTENTS OF THE BIBLE

OLD TESTAMENT: 39 BOOKS

I. *Law:* 5 BOOKS

Genesis, Exodus, Leviticus, Numbers, Deuteronomy

II. *History:* 12 BOOKS

Joshua, Judges, Ruth, 1 and 2 Samuel, 1 and 2 Kings, 1 and 2 Chronicles, Ezra, Nehemiah, Esther

III. *Poetry:* 5 BOOKS

Job, Psalms, Proverbs, Ecclesiastes, Song of Solomon

IV. *Prophecy:* 17 BOOKS

The Major Prophets: 5 BOOKS
Isaiah, Jeremiah, Lamentations, Ezekiel, Daniel

The Minor Prophets: 12 BOOKS

Hosea, Joel, Amos, Obadiah, Jonah, Micah, Nahum, Habakkuk, Zephaniah, Haggai, Zechariah, Malachi

NEW TESTAMENT: 27 BOOKS

I. *Historical:* 5 BOOKS

Matthew, Mark, Luke, John, Acts

II. *Epistles or Doctrinal:* 21 BOOKS

Romans, 1 and 2 Corinthians, Galatians, Ephesians, Philippians, Colossians, 1 and 2 Thessalonians, 1 and 2 Timothy, Titus, Philemon, Hebrews, James, 1 and 2 Peter, 1, 2 and 3 John, Jude

III. *Apocalyptic:* 1 BOOK

Revelation

CHAPTER 15

Memorizing Bible Passages

A frequent criticism leveled against the church schools today is that the children do little or no memorizing. All lovers of the Bible will agree that it is indeed deplorable when boys and girls grow to adulthood without having stored away in memory many of the superbly beautiful Bible passages that have been the spiritual food of generations.

Parents are completely right in feeling that there is high value here that should somehow be secured for the children. But memorization also has its dangers. If the process of memorizing is an irksome task, imposed on the child by someone without regard to his own desire or interest, if in the midst of the process he is resentful and bored, and if he learns to dislike the very words he is repeating because they are associated with a situation that to him is unpleasant, it is hard to believe that the net result can be satisfactory. The parents' real aim is not accomplished.

On the other hand, if the child's own desire to memorize a passage is stimulated, if he shares with his parents a deep appreciation of the selected verses, if he associates with the use of the words a warm and happy feeling of family fellowship, and if he sees a reason for the memorizing that makes sense to him, then the memorizing will probably be well and speedily accomplished.

PARENTS' INTEREST AND EXAMPLE

Here, as in so many other instances, the example of the parents can provide an effective stimulus. "Dad and Mother have decided to learn these verses by heart. We like to think about them and say them to ourselves sometimes when we don't have the Bible in our hands. We're going to read them over aloud every day this week at breakfast time (lunch? dinner? bedtime?) and then see if by Sunday we know them."

Given a wise selection of verses, and careful discussion of unfamiliar words or ideas, it will not be surprising if the children learn the passage by heart before the parents do! Obviously, the selections will be partly determined by what the parents' own favorite passages are. As a beginning it will probably be wise to limit the amount to two or three verses, perhaps Psalms 90:1-2, Psalms 46:1-3, Mark 12:28-31. Later, parts of the thirteenth chapter of 1 Corinthians would surely be included. Many people like to conclude these verses with the first four words of the fourteenth chapter: "Make love your aim."

The family Bible could be left open to the passage with the chosen verses marked (when the children are old enough to read) or a copy of the selection could be put on a family bulletin board for ready reference in between readings.

CHURCH SCHOOL SUGGESTIONS

Once a family becomes accustomed to this activity frequent reasons will be found for engaging in it. Practically all church schools send home at times suggestions for memory work. It can be a pleasant experience to learn these *as a family*, each one helping the others and all discussing the meaning and sharing in appreciation.

In Preparation for Christmas. How fine a preparation for Christmas it would be to memorize the Nativity stories (Luke 2:8-20; Matthew 2:1-11) during Advent and be able to repeat them together when the crêche is set up! As a variation, different members of the family may recite the parts (angel, shepherds, wise men, Herod) while one member carries the narrative. Perhaps the whole family might sing the angels' chorus at the appropriate place in the story.

In Preparation for Thanksgiving. A memorized psalm, or part of one, repeated in unison, makes an appropriate and meaningful grace for the Thanksgiving family dinner. Or each member of the family may choose a "thankful verse"; these may be repeated in turn, and the family may unite in a selected prayer verse for the conclusion (such as Psalms 75:1).

Several weeks before Thanksgiving the family may make their plans, and choose the verses or passages to be learned. Copying the verses on cards, or marking the passage in the Bible in some way for ready reference may facilitate the learning.

A number of appropriate selections are given here, but of course the choice need not be limited to these.

I will give thanks to the Lord with my whole heart;
    I will tell of all thy wonderful deeds.
I will be glad and exult in thee,
    I will sing praise to thy name, O Most High.

PSALMS 9:1

O come, let us sing to the Lord;
    let us make a joyful noise to the rock of our salvation!
Let us come before his presence with thanksgiving;
    let us make a joyful noise to him with songs of praise!
For the Lord is a great God,
    and a great King above all gods.

PSALMS 95:1–3

It is good to give thanks to the Lord,
    to sing praises to thy name, O Most High;
to declare thy steadfast love in the morning,
    and thy faithfulness by night,
to the music of the lute and the harp,
    to the melody of the lyre.

For thou, O Lord, hast made me glad by thy work;
  at the works of thy hands I sing for joy.

How great are thy works, O Lord!
  Thy thoughts are very deep!

                                    PSALMS 92:1–5

Sing praises to the Lord, O you his saints,
  and give thanks to his holy name.
For his anger is but for a moment,
  and his favor is for a lifetime.
Weeping may tarry for the night,
  but joy comes with the morning.

                                    PSALMS 30:4–5

[God says]: He who brings thanksgiving as his sacrifice
    honors me.

                                    PSALMS 50:23

We give thanks to thee, O God; we give thanks;
  we call on thy name and recount thy wondrous deeds.

                                    PSALMS 75:1

I give thanks to thee, O Lord my God, with my whole
    heart,
  and I will glorify thy name for ever.
For great is thy steadfast love toward me.

                                    PSALMS 86:12–13

I will sing to the Lord as long as I live;
  I will sing praise to my God while I have being.

                                    PSALMS 104:33

A MEMORY GAME

Parents and children together may make a set of cards, the
parents printing or typing selected Bible verses on one side,
and the children adding a reminder illustration of each verse
on the back. These illustrations may be drawn or clipped
from magazines and pasted on. Suggested verses that lend
themselves to this treatment are listed below. Others will occur to the family as the game develops.

When the cards have been prepared, the game may be played as follows: The cards are placed in a pile, picture side up. Each player in turn draws the top card from the pile, keeping it picture side up on the table in front of him. If he can repeat the verse on the back of the card from memory, he keeps the card and draws another, continuing until he fails to know the verse, at which time the card is placed in the center of the table, picture side up. The next player may either draw a card from the top of the pile or from the center of the table. When all the cards have been distributed, the player having the most cards wins. New cards may be added from time to time as members of the family discover appropriate verses.

Tree:	Genesis 1:12; Psalms 1:3; 96:12; 104:16; Matthew 7:17
House:	Matthew 7:24; Psalms 127:1
Birds:	Psalms 104:12, 17; Matthew 6:26; 10:29, 31; Jeremiah 8:7
Flowers:	Matthew 6:28–29; Song of Solomon 2:12
Sun:	Psalms 104:19; Matthew 5:45
Snow:	Job 37:6
Rain:	Matthew 5:45; Job 37:6
Crowds of people:	Matthew 9:36; 14:14
Animals:	Genesis 1:24; Psalms 104:14
Mountains:	Psalms 90:2; 95:4; 104:8; 46:2–3; 125:2
Sea:	Psalms 95:5; 104:25; 46:2–3
Sheep:	Psalms 23:1; Matthew 12:11
Hills:	Psalms 121:1–2; 24:3–4
Church:	Psalms 122:1
Springs, brooks:	Psalms 104:10
City:	Matthew 5:14; Psalms 127:1
Grass:	Matthew 6:30

After the family have learned a number of verses, they may enjoy an adaptation of this game without the cards, when they are taking a trip or a long ride in the family car, the game being to hunt for reminders of the Bible verses, and repeat the appropriate verses in unison.

Other suggestions for memorizing have been offered in Chapter 9.

CHAPTER 16

Conflicting Ideas of God

In a previous chapter a number of Bible stories are mentioned in which troublesome elements occur. Many of these are so familiar to us that we are a little shocked, when we approach them from the standpoint of a small child, to realize what savage, bloodthirsty incidents many of them contain.

Difficult as these stories of primitive human relations are, some of the Old Testament materials present even greater problems—greater because in them lies a grave danger to the child's relationship to God. These are the stories and passages which embody primitive, pre-Christian ideas of God. It is well to remind ourselves that beneath all our efforts to nurture our children in the Christian faith lies the basic need to help them develop a personal relationship to God—God as Jesus knew him and revealed him.

God, as portrayed in the New Testament, is primarily a God of love. He is like a loving Father. Who, having once read it, can forget the picture Jesus painted in his story of the Prodigal Son? It has sometimes been more appropriately called the "Parable of the Forgiving Father." (Luke 15:11–24)

God's love according to Jesus, in addition to being like that of a loving Father, is impartial and is given to each person without his earning or deserving it.

He makes his sun rise on the evil and on the good, and sends rain on the just and on the unjust.

MATTHEW 5:45

His love actively reaches out to find and restore evil-doers. Jesus said:

What man of you, having a hundred sheep, if he has lost one of them, does not leave the ninety-nine in the wilderness, and go after the one which is lost, until he finds it? And when he has found it, he lays it on his shoulders, rejoicing. And when he comes home, he calls together his friends and his neighbors, saying to them, "Rejoice with me, for I have found my sheep which was lost." Just so, I tell you, there will be more joy in heaven over one sinner who repents than over ninety-nine righteous persons who need no repentance.

LUKE 15:4–7

This loving Father God is ready to bestow "good gifts" on those who will accept them. This is not to be misunderstood as suggesting that God is a glorified Santa Claus—the good gifts are spiritual, not material.

Ask, and it will be given you; seek and you will find; knock, and it will be opened to you. For every one who asks receives, and he who seeks finds, and to him who knocks it will be opened. Or what man of you, if his son asks him for bread, will give him a stone? Or if he asks for a fish, will give him a serpent? If you then, who are evil, know how to give good gifts to your children, how much more will your Father who is in heaven give good things to those who ask him?

MATTHEW 7:7–11

God's love for us is steady, dependable, patient, unchanging. No one has given a better picture of its trustworthiness than Paul in these unforgettable verses from his Epistle to the Romans:

Who shall separate us from the love of Christ? Shall tribulation, or distress, or persecution, or famine, or nakedness, or peril, or sword? . . . No, in all these things we are more than conquerors through him who loved us. For I am sure that neither death, nor life, nor angels, nor principalities, nor things present,

nor things to come, nor powers, nor height, nor depth, nor anything else in all creation, will be able to separate us from the love
of God in Christ Jesus our Lord.

ROMANS 8:35–39

Turning from this conception of God as depicted in the
New Testament to the pages of the Old Testament, the reader
finds himself in a totally different spiritual atmosphere. Here
are frequently found ideas of God in direct conflict with the
Christian conceptions. Consider the following passages.

A destructive God. In the early parts of Genesis is the story
of the Flood.

> The Lord saw that the wickedness of man was great in the
> earth, and that every imagination of the thoughts of his heart
> was only evil continually. . . . So the Lord said, "I will blot out
> man whom I have created from the face of the ground, man and
> beast and creeping things and birds of the air, for I am sorry
> that I have made them." . . . And the waters prevailed so might-
> ily upon the earth that all the high mountains under the whole
> heaven were covered. . . . And all flesh died that moved upon
> the earth, birds, cattle, beasts, all swarming creatures that swarm
> upon the earth, and every man. . . . He blotted out every living
> thing that was upon the face of the ground, man and animals and
> creeping things and birds of the air; they were blotted out from
> the earth.

GENESIS 6:5, 7; 7:19, 21, 23

> Then the Lord rained on Sodom and Gomorrah brimstone and
> fire from the Lord out of heaven; and he overthrew those cities,
> and all the valley, and all the inhabitants of the cities. . . . And
> lo, the smoke of the land went up like the smoke of a furnace.

GENESIS 19:24–25, 28

A jealous God.

> . . . for I the Lord your God am a jealous God, visiting the
> iniquity of the fathers upon the children to the third and the
> fourth generation of those who hate me.

EXODUS 20:5

A merciless God.

> And the Lord said to Moses, "Bring out of the camp him who
> cursed . . . and let all the congregation stone him. And say to

the people of Israel . . . He who blasphemes the name of the Lord shall be put to death. . . . When a man causes a disfigurement in his neighbor, as he has done it shall be done to him, fracture for fracture, eye for eye, tooth for tooth; as he has disfigured a man, he shall be disfigured."

LEVITICUS 24:13–20

It is interesting to compare this passage with one in Matthew:

[Jesus said] "You have heard that it was said, 'An eye for an eye and a tooth for a tooth.' But I say to you, Do not resist one who is evil. But if any one strikes you on the right cheek, turn to him the other also . . ."

MATTHEW 5:38–39

A threatening God.

If you walk in my statutes and observe my commandments and do them, then . . . I will walk among you, and will be your God, and you shall be my people. I am the Lord your God. . . . But if you will not hearken to me, and will not do all these commandments . . . then I will walk contrary to you in fury, and chastise you myself sevenfold for your sins. You shall eat the flesh of your sons, and you shall eat the flesh of your daughters. And I will destroy your high places, and cut down your incense altars, and cast your dead bodies upon the dead bodies of your idols; and my soul will abhor you.

LEVITICUS 26:3, 12, 14, 28–30

A vengeful God.

And the Lord said to Moses, "Say to the congregation, Get away from about the dwelling of Korah, Dathan and Abiram." . . . So they got away . . . and Dathan and Abiram came out and stood at the door of their tents, together with their wives, their sons, and their little ones. . . . And . . . the ground under them split asunder; and the earth opened its mouth and swallowed them up, with their households and all the men that belonged to Korah and all their goods.

NUMBERS 16:23–24, 27, 31–32

An unforgiving God.

Now this is the commandment, the statutes and the ordinances which the Lord your God commanded me to teach you. . . . If a man has a stubborn and rebellious son, who will not obey the voice of his father or the voice of his mother, and, though they chastise him, will not give heed to them, then his father and his mother shall take hold of him and bring him out to the elders of his city at the gate of the place where he lives, and they shall say to the elders of his city, "This our son is stubborn and rebellious, he will not obey our voice; he is a glutton and a drunkard." Then all the men of the city shall stone him to death with stones.

DEUTERONOMY 6:1; 21:18–21

A cruel God.

And Samuel said to Saul . . . "Thus says the Lord of hosts, 'I will punish what Amalek did to Israel in opposing them on the way, when they came up out of Egypt. Now go and smite Amalek, and utterly destroy all that they have; do not spare them, but kill both man and woman, infant and suckling, ox and sheep, camel and ass.' "

1 SAMUEL 15:1–3

A spiteful God.

[Elisha] went up from there to Bethel; and while he was going up on the way, some small boys came out of the city and jeered at him, saying, "Go up, you baldhead! Go up, you baldhead!" And he turned around, and when he saw them, he cursed them in the name of the Lord. And two she-bears came out of the woods and tore forty-two of the boys.

2 KINGS 2:23–24

A pitiless God.

Thus says the Lord God: Behold, I, even I, am against you; and I will execute judgments in the midst of you in the sight of the nations. And because of all your abominations I will do with you what I have never yet done, and the like of which I will never do again. . . . Wherefore, as I live, says the Lord God, surely, because you have defiled my sanctuary with all your detestable things and with all your abominations, therefore I will cut you down; my eye will not spare, and I will have no pity. A third part of you shall die of pestilence and be consumed with famine in the midst of you; a third part shall fall by the sword round about you; and a third part I will scatter to all the winds and will unsheathe the sword after them. Thus shall my anger spend itself,

and I will vent my fury upon them and satisfy myself; and they
shall know that I, the Lord, have spoken in my jealousy, when I
spend my fury upon them.

EZEKIEL 5:8–13

A God like a beast.

I am the Lord your God
  from the land of Egypt;
you know no God but me,
  and besides me there is no savior.
It was I who knew you in the wilderness,
  in the land of drought;
but when they had fed to the full,
  they were filled, and their heart was lifted up;
  therefore they forgot me.
So I will be to them like a lion,
  like a leopard I will lurk beside the way.
I will fall upon them like a bear robbed of her cubs,
  I will tear open their breast,
and there I will devour them like a lion,
  as a wild beast would rend them.

HOSEA 13:4–8

These few examples, selected almost at random from the
pages of the Old Testament, could be multiplied many times.
These are sufficient, however, to indicate the danger to a
child's developing faith in "the God and Father of our Lord
Jesus Christ." (Ephesians 1:3) Parents will need to be ready
to explain that in the early days people had not yet come to
understand God clearly; that many different and often contradictory concepts of God are in the Bible; and that for us
as Christians all ideas of God are tested by the revelation of
God in Jesus. We accept as true in the Old Testament only
those concepts of God consistent with his revelation in Christ.

As the writer of the Epistle to the Hebrews puts it:

God, who gave to our forefathers many different glimpses of
the truth in the words of the prophets, has now, at the end of the
present age, given us the truth in the Son.[1]

[1] Hebrews 1:1–2 from *The New Testament in Modern English*, Copyright
J. B. Phillips 1958. Used by permission of The Macmillan Company and
Geoffrey Bles Ltd., London.

Incarnate in Jesus, God revealed himself fully. In the radiance of embodied love, despised, rejected, crucified, but holding steadfast to its essential nature in spite of the worst that hatred and evil could do—here men could behold in awed reverence the heart of God himself. In Christ all the misconceptions about God in the Old Testament were revealed as untrue, and all the glimmerings of truth were confirmed and magnified.

Once this point of view has been firmly grasped the pre-Christian conceptions of God in the Old Testament present no serious difficulty. It is easy to say, "This is how men thought at that time, *but Jesus taught* ————." Or, "God was not really like that, but men had not yet come to understand him. When Jesus came, he showed us what God is really like."

The whole point of view emphasizes again the point made in Chapter 13 that Old Testament material must be considered and evaluated in the light of the New.

The repeated "Thus saith the Lord" needs to be understood and interpreted as one man's sincere but sometimes mistaken attempt to speak for God. Dr. Rufus Jones says:

> It is high time that we should seriously realize that vital religion cannot be maintained and preserved on the theory that God dealt with our human race only in the far past ages, and that the Bible is the only evidence we have that our God is *a living, revealing, communicating God*. If God ever spoke, He is still speaking. If He has ever been in mutual and reciprocal communication with the persons He has made, He is still a communicating God, as eager as ever to have listening and receptive souls. If there is something of His image and superscription in our inmost structure and being, we ought to expect a continuous revelation of His will and purpose through the ages. . . . He is the *Great I Am*, not a Great He was.[2]

Although many of the conceptions of the Old Testament people were mistaken, their struggle to understand bore pre-

[2] Rufus M. Jones, *A Call to What Is Vital* (New York: The Macmillan Company, 1948), p. 65.

cious fruit indeed as the centuries passed. Always to some few, stretching their minds and hearts for deeper understanding, God was able to reveal himself ever more truly and clearly. Dr. Fosdick sums up the amazing development of the idea of God in the following revealing paragraphs:

> In retrospect, the road traveled by the idea of God through the Bible as a whole presents a fascinating spectacle.
>
> Beginning with a storm god on a desert mountain, it ends with men saying "God is a spirit: and they that worship him must worship in spirit and in truth." (John 4:24)
>
> Beginning with a tribal war god, leading his devotees to bloody triumph over their foes, it ends with men seeing that "God is love; and he that abideth in love abideth in God, and God abideth in him." (1 John 4:16)
>
> Beginning with a territorial deity who loved his clansmen and hated the remainder of mankind, it ends with a great multitude out of every tribe and tongue and people and nation (Revelation 5:9) worshipping one universal Father.
>
> Beginning with a god who walked in a garden in the cool of the day or who showed his back to Moses as a special favor, it ends with the God whom "no man hath seen . . . at any time" (John 1:18) and in whom "we live, and move, and have our being." (Acts 17:28)
>
> Beginning with a god who commanded the slaughter of infants and sucklings without mercy, it ends with the God whose will it is that not "One of these little ones should perish." (Matthew 18:14)
>
> Beginning with a god from whom at Sinai the people shrank in fear, saying, "Let not God speak with us, lest we die" (Exodus 20:19; cf. Deuteronomy 5:25), it ends with the God to whom one prays in the solitary place and whose indwelling Spirit is our unseen friend.
>
> Beginning with a god whose highest social vision was a tribal victory, it ends with the God whose worshippers pray for a world-wide kingdom of righteousness and peace.[3]

[3] Harry Emerson Fosdick, *A Guide to Understanding the Bible* (New York: Harper & Row, Publishers, Incorporated), pp. 53–54.

CHAPTER 17

Revelations of God Through the Prophets

In the previous chapter attention was called to pre-Christian
ideas of God found in the pages of the Old Testament. It is
important for anyone dealing with children as they read the
Bible to be aware of these stumbling blocks to a wholesome
relationship to God. It is not surprising that primitive ideas
of God should be found among the early peoples of whom
the Old Testament tells. The surprising thing is that even in
those early days men occasionally caught flashes of revelation
regarding the true nature of God, and proclaimed these truths
with complete fearlessness and disregard of consequences.

It would be unfair to leave the consideration of various
ideas of God in the Old Testament without some mention
of a few of these fearless and inspired leaders, the prophets,
whose understandings of God's true nature at their highest
and best came close to the teachings of Jesus, and laid the
foundation for his complete and perfect revelation.

> In the goodly fellowship of the prophets we meet with a reli-
> gious phenomenon unique and without parallel. Here we have
> to deal with one of the profound movements of the human spirit
> and with the most significant aspect of Old Testament revelation.
> Prophets there have been in other religions and in other times,
> but nowhere do we find a comparable succession of mighty crea-

tive personalities who linked the prophetic impulse to spiritual religion and made the religion of Israel a permanent force in the world and a real preparation for the Christian gospel.[1]

> The fundamental belief of the prophets is their belief in the living God. . . . This God, too, is holy and righteous altogether. He demands righteousness and justice from his people. Evil, cruelty, and oppression he abhors, and he is deeply concerned for the sufferings of the poor and needy. . . . Here is expressed a flaming passion against all forms of social injustice, and from those prophets social reformers have never ceased to draw strength and inspiration.[2]

The prophets were constantly denouncing the distorted ideas of God that were prevalent in their times. Contrast with the idea of a revengeful God "visiting the iniquities of the fathers upon the children to the third and fourth generation" this passage from Ezekiel:

> The word of the Lord came to me again: "What do you mean by repeating this proverb concerning the land of Israel, 'The fathers have eaten sour grapes, and the children's teeth are set on edge'? As I live, says the Lord God, this proverb shall no more be used by you in Israel. Behold, all souls are mine; the soul of the father as well as the soul of the son is mine. . . . The son shall not suffer for the iniquity of the father, nor the father suffer for the iniquity of the son; the righteousness of the righteous shall be upon himself, and the wickedness of the wicked shall be upon himself." Ezekiel 18:1–4, 20 (This entire chapter is given to an amplification of this idea.)

A number of the prophets speak out against the idea that God could ever be satisfied with mere ceremonial observances. Amos declares:

> For thus says the Lord to the house of Israel:
> "Seek me and live;
>   but do not seek Bethel,
>   and do not enter into Gilgal
>   or cross over to Beer-sheba . . ."

[1] John Paterson, *The Goodly Fellowship of the Prophets* (New York: Charles Scribner's Sons, 1948), p. 1.
[2] *Ibid.*, pp. 8–9.

(These three places were sanctuaries for the worship of Yahweh. Amos is thus protesting against the debased, "externalized" forms of worship prevalent at that time, and, in the passage below, pleading for the reality of inner righteousness expressing itself in acts of mercy and justice.)

> Hate evil, and love good,
>> and establish justice in the gate.
>
> . . .
>
> I hate, I despise your feasts,
>> and I take no delight in your solemn assemblies.
> Even though you offer me your burnt offerings and
> cereal offerings,
>> I will not accept them,
> and the peace offerings of your fatted beasts
>> I will not look upon.
> Take away from me the noise of your songs;
>> to the melody of your harps I will not listen.
> But let justice roll down like waters,
>> and righteousness like an ever-flowing stream.
>> AMOS 5:4–5, 15, 21–24

Micah speaks in no uncertain terms as to God's requirements of man:

> With what shall I come before the Lord,
>> and bow myself before God on high?
> Shall I come before him with burnt offerings,
>> with calves a year old?
> Will the Lord be pleased with thousands of rams,
>> with ten thousands of rivers of oil?
> Shall I give my first-born for my transgression,
>> the fruit of my body for the sin of my soul?
> He has showed you, O man, what is good;
>> and what does the Lord require of you
> but to do justice, and to love kindness,
>> and to walk humbly with your God?
>> MICAH 6:6–8

Isaiah, too, pleads for righteousness as the offering most pleasing to God:

> Hear the word of the Lord . . .
> Give ear to the teaching of our God! . . .
> "What to me is the multitude of your sacrifices?"
>> says the Lord;
> "I have had enough of burnt offering of rams
>> and the fat of fed beasts;
> I do not delight in the blood of bulls,
>> or of lambs, or of he-goats.
>
> "When you come to appear before me,
>> who requires of you
>> this trampling of my courts?
> Bring no more vain offerings;
>> incense is an abomination to me.
> New moon and sabbath and the calling of assemblies—
>> I cannot endure iniquity and solemn assembly.
> Your new moons and your appointed feasts
>> my soul hates;
> they have become a burden to me,
>> I am weary of bearing them.
> When you spread forth your hands,
>> I will hide my eyes from you;
> even though you make many prayers,
>> I will not listen;
>> your hands are full of blood.
> Wash yourselves; make yourselves clean;
>> remove the evil of your doings
>> from before my eyes;
> cease to do evil,
>> learn to do good;
> seek justice,
>> correct oppression;
> defend the fatherless,
>> plead for the widow."

ISAIAH 1:10–17

In this connection the words of Paul written many years later seem to sum up all the protests of the prophets against meaningless "sacrifices" and add a new note that speaks directly to our hearts today:

I appeal to you therefore, brethren, by the mercies of God, to present your bodies as a living sacrifice, holy and acceptable to God, which is your spiritual worship. (Romans 12:1)

Lastly the unnamed prophet in the book of Isaiah says:

Cry aloud, spare not,
> lift up your voice like a trumpet;
declare to my people their transgression . . .
Behold, you fast only to quarrel and to fight
> and to hit with wicked fist.
Fasting like yours this day
> will not make your voice to be heard on high.
Is such the fast that I choose,
> a day for a man to humble himself?
Is it to bow down his head like a rush,
> and to spread sackcloth and ashes under him?
Will you call this a fast,
> and a day acceptable to the Lord?
Is not this the fast that I choose:
> to loose the bonds of wickedness,
> to undo the thongs of the yoke,
to let the oppressed go free,
> and to break every yoke?
Is it not to share your bread with the hungry,
> and bring the homeless poor into your house;
when you see the naked, to cover him,
> and not to hide yourself from your own flesh?
Then shall your light break forth like the dawn,
> and your healing shall spring up speedily;
your righteousness shall go before you,
> the glory of the Lord shall be your rear guard.
Then you shall call, and the Lord will answer;
> you shall cry, and he will say, Here I am.
>   ISAIAH 58:1, 4–9

This same prophet is the author of the familiar passage below:

Seek the Lord while he may be found,
> call upon him while he is near;
let the wicked forsake his way,
> and the unrighteous man his thoughts;
let him return to the Lord, that he may have mercy on him,
> and to our God, for he will abundantly pardon.

For my thoughts are not your thoughts,
　　neither are your ways my ways, says the Lord,
For as the heavens are higher than the earth,
　　so are my ways higher than your ways
　　and my thoughts than your thoughts.

For as the rain and the snow come down from heaven,
　　and return not thither but water the earth,
making it bring forth and sprout,
　　giving seed to the sower and bread to the eater,
so shall my word be that goes forth from my mouth;
　　it shall not return to me empty,
but it shall accomplish that which I purpose,
　　and prosper in the thing for which I sent it.

ISAIAH 55:6–11

Two Old Testament books voice a protest against the narrow interpretation of the "chosen people" as one more loved by God than other peoples.

The book of Ruth tells the story of a Moabitess (a foreigner) who becomes a beloved member of the Jewish group, and in the course of time an ancestress of King David and of Jesus. Few more beautiful descriptions of human love can be found than Ruth's words to Naomi:

"Entreat me not to leave you or to return from following you; for where you go I will go, and where you lodge I will lodge; your people shall be my people, and your God my God; where you die I will die, and there will I be buried." (Ruth 1:16–17)

The story is a moving sermon showing love transcending all barriers of race or class or nationality.

The second book mentioned above is the book of Jonah. This brief but powerful story has suffered much because literal-minded people have refused to believe it "true" that Jonah could be swallowed by a whale and still live. And so the tremendous truth in the story has been neglected. This is not a story to be read as literal fact. It is instead a parable—"a powerful plea for love toward an enemy country."[3]

---

[3] Rufus M. Jones, *A Call to What Is Vital* (New York: The Macmillan Company, 1948), p. 10.

The whole point of the story is that Jonah, receiving God's orders to go to Nineveh and "cry against it" because of its wickedness, wants no part in such a mission. He refuses to obey, and flees "from the presence of the Lord" in the opposite direction, setting sail in a boat from Joppa, intending to go to Tarshish.

> But the Lord hurled a great wind upon the sea, and there was a mighty tempest on the sea, so that the ship threatened to break up. (Jonah 1:4)

The sailors cast lots to know who is responsible for their misfortune and the lot falls upon Jonah. So it is that Jonah finds himself thrown into the sea, where "the Lord appointed a great fish to swallow" him; and eventually, having duly repented in the body of the fish, Jonah is cast up safe and sound upon dry land.

A second time God orders Jonah to go to Nineveh, and this time he obeys. He cries against the city so persuasively that the people believe him when he threatens the city's destruction. And the king orders all the people to repent in sackcloth and ashes, to "cry mightily to God" and to turn from their evil ways. And God sees the result of Jonah's mission and decides to spare the city.

But Jonah is angry! He goes outside the city to wait and see what will happen. There is a certain quaintness in the end of the story:

> And the Lord God appointed a plant, and made it come up over Jonah, that it might be a shade over his head, to save him from his discomfort. So Jonah was exceedingly glad because of the plant. But when dawn came up the next day, God appointed a worm which attacked the plant, so that it withered. When the sun rose, God appointed a sultry east wind, and the sun beat upon the head of Jonah so that he was faint; and he asked that he might die, and said, "It is better for me to die than to live." But God said to Jonah, "Do you do well to be angry for the plant?" And he said, "I do well to be angry, angry enough to die." And the Lord said, "You pity the plant, for which you did not labor, nor did you make it grow, which came into being in a night, and

perished in a night. And should not I pity Nineveh, that great
city, in which there are more than a hundred and twenty thousand persons who do not know their right hand from their left,
and also much cattle?" (Jonah 4:6–11)

So ends an unknown prophet's revelation of God's concern
for "foreigners" as well as for the Hebrews.

In these two stories we have the beginning conception of a
universal God, of the "one flock, one shepherd" idea of
Jesus. (John 10:16)

> And men will come from east and west, and from north and
> south, and sit at table in the kingdom of God. (Luke 13:29)

In yet another place the Old Testament envisions the whole
world united in the worship of the living God:

> It shall come to pass in the latter days
>   that the mountain of the house of the Lord
> shall be established as the highest of the mountains,
>   and shall be raised up above the hills;
> and peoples shall flow to it,
>   and many nations shall come and say:
> "Come, let us go up to the mountain of the Lord,
>   to the house of the God of Jacob;
> that he may teach us his ways
>   and we may walk in his paths."
> For out of Zion shall go forth the law,
>   and the word of the Lord from Jerusalem.
> He shall judge between many peoples,
>   and shall decide for strong nations afar off;
> and they shall beat their swords into plowshares,
>   and their spears into pruning-hooks;
> nation shall not lift up sword against nation,
>   neither shall they learn war any more;
> but they shall sit every man under his vine and under
>   his fig tree,
>   and none shall make them afraid;
>   for the mouth of the Lord of hosts has spoken.
>   MICAH 4:1–4

CHAPTER 18

Revelations of God in the Psalms

One other Old Testament book rises to heights of grandeur in some of its ideas of God—the book of Psalms. This ancient hymnbook has spoken to the hearts of men in all generations. Here are despairing prayers, ecstatic hymns of joy, pleadings for understanding, urgent cries to God for help, and quiet, profound affirmations of faith in the midst of life's difficulties and confusions. Over and over again as we read the Psalms, we find the Psalmist's words voicing our own deepest needs and aspirations.

Because the Psalms came from the hearts of many different people, and out of many different situations, here, too, are to be found vast differences of spiritual insight. Not every psalm embodies a Christian idea of God; some are savage prayers for revenge on enemies. The reader, however, who keeps in mind the Christian conception of God already referred to at some length in Chapter 16 can find in the Psalms deeply satisfying thoughts of God's goodness and "steadfast love."

Here are a few passages that have been loved by people of all generations:

The heavens are telling the glory of God;
    and the firmament proclaims his handiwork.
Day to day pours forth speech,
    and night to night declares knowledge.

There is no speech, nor are there words;
    their voice is not heard;
yet their voice goes out through all the earth,
    and their words to the end of the world.

PSALMS 19:1–4

The law of the Lord is perfect,
    reviving the soul;
the testimony of the Lord is sure,
    making wise the simple;
the precepts of the Lord are right,
    rejoicing the heart;
the commandment of the Lord is pure,
    enlightening the eyes;
the fear of the Lord is clean,
    enduring for ever;
the ordinances of the Lord are true,
    and righteous altogether.

PSALMS 19:7–9

God is our refuge and strength,
    a very present help in trouble.
Therefore we will not fear though the earth should change,
    though the mountains shake in the heart of the sea;
though its waters roar and foam,
    though the mountains tremble with its tumult.

PSALMS 46:1–3

The Lord is merciful and gracious,
    slow to anger and abounding in steadfast love.
He will not always chide,
    nor will he keep his anger for ever.
He does not deal with us according to our sins,
    nor requite us according to our iniquities.
For as the heavens are high above the earth,
    so great is his steadfast love toward those who fear him;
as far as the east is from the west,
    so far does he remove our transgressions from us.
As a father pities his children,
    so the Lord pities those who fear him.
For he knows our frame;
    he remembers that we are dust.

As for man, his days are like grass;
    he flourishes like a flower of the field;
for the wind passes over it, and it is gone,
    and its place knows it no more.
But the steadfast love of the Lord is from everlasting
        to everlasting
    upon those who fear him,
    and his righteousness to children's children,
to those who keep his covenant
    and remember to do his commandments.

PSALMS 103:8–18

Lord, thou hast been our dwelling place
    in all generations.
Before the mountains were brought forth,
    or ever thou hadst formed the earth and the world,
    from everlasting to everlasting thou art God.

PSALMS 90:1–2

Whither shall I go from thy Spirit?
    or whither shall I flee from thy presence?
If I ascend to heaven, thou art there!
    If I make my bed in Sheol, thou art there!
If I take the wings of the morning
    and dwell in the uttermost parts of the sea,
even there thy hand shall lead me,
    and thy right hand shall hold me.
If I say, "Let only darkness cover me,
    and the light about me be night,"
even the darkness is not dark to thee,
    the night is bright as the day;
    for darkness is as light with thee.

PSALMS 139:7–12

Those who trust in the Lord are like Mount Zion,
    which cannot be moved, but abides forever.
As the mountains are round about Jerusalem,
    so the Lord is round about his people,
    from this time forth and for evermore.

PSALMS 125:1–2

O Lord, our Lord,
  how majestic is thy name in all the earth!

                    . . .

When I look at thy heavens, the work of thy fingers,
  the moon and the stars which thou hast established;
what is man that thou art mindful of him,
  and the son of man that thou dost care for him?

Yet thou hast made him little less than God,
  and dost crown him with glory and honor.
Thou hast given him dominion over the works of thy hands;
  thou hast put all things under his feet,
all sheep and oxen,
  and also the beasts of the field,
the birds of the air, and the fish of the sea,
  whatever passes along the paths of the sea.

O Lord, our Lord,
  how majestic is thy name in all the earth!

                                    PSALMS 8:1, 3–9

The Lord is my light and my salvation;
  whom shall I fear?
The Lord is the stronghold of my life;
  of whom shall I be afraid?

One thing have I asked of the Lord,
  that will I seek after;
that I may dwell in the house of the Lord
  all the days of my life,
to behold the beauty of the Lord,
  and to inquire in his temple.

                                    PSALMS 27:1, 4

Rejoice in the Lord, O you righteous!
Praise befits the upright.
Praise the Lord with the lyre,
  make melody to him with the harp of ten strings!

For the word of the Lord is upright;
  and all his work is done in faithfulness,
He loves righteousness and justice;
  the earth is full of the steadfast love of the Lord.

                                    PSALMS 33:1–2, 4–5

Thy steadfast love, O Lord, extends to the heavens,
    thy faithfulness to the clouds.
Thy righteousness is like the mountains of God,
    thy judgments are like the great deep;
    man and beast thou savest, O Lord.

How precious is thy steadfast love, O God!
    The children of men take refuge in
        the shadow of thy wings.
They feast on the abundance of thy house,
    and thou givest them drink from the river
        of thy delights.
For with thee is the fountain of life;
    in thy light do we see light.

O continue thy steadfast love to those who know thee,
    and thy salvation to the upright of heart!

PSALMS 36:5–10

CHAPTER 19

Nativity Stories and Miracles

In previous chapters some of the difficulties inherent in the Old Testament have been faced. An effort has been made to show how the New Testament revelation grew out of the religious insights of the Old but went far beyond them. It was suggested that parents will do well to see the Old Testament always in the light of New Testament ideas, being alert to protect children from pre-Christian ideas of God.

The problems of Biblical literature, however, are not limited to the Old Testament. The New Testament, too, has its difficult passages, its obscure meanings, its controversial material. It is very necessary for parents to be prepared to meet the questions the children will almost certainly raise as they broaden their knowledge of the Gospels and other New Testament writings.

The reader is reminded that, concerning the matters under discussion, different points of view are held by equally sincere Christians. No one can claim final and definitive answers that will seem right to everyone. If the comments and suggestions in these chapters are not in accord with your considered beliefs, they may at least serve the purpose of pointing out places where children will need help.

Rufus Jones has cautioned us that it is well to beware of allowing the questions to assume undue importance. He says:

The interrogation point has been written all over the documents that transmit the facts to us, and we have missed the *exclamation point*—the glory and the wonder.[1]

It is the author's feeling that the "wonder and the glory" are best maintained by frank and honest facing of the difficulties as they arise. Parents may enter with the children into the search for answers, may *wonder with* them, stimulating their further quest for the truth, may kindle in them a recognition of the vast mysteries that challenge our upreaching minds and hearts.

Sometimes this approach may mean that the belief in a literal interpretation of some specific story may be changed into reverence for sacred symbolism.

Sometimes it may mean that the child's conclusions will not coincide with the parent's. We must never lose sight of the fact that each individual must do his own thinking. A child who accepts without thought or question the belief presented to him is merely postponing a necessary process to later years. Only as he has thought and tested, and rethought and retested his ideas and beliefs, can he possibly achieve a faith of his own. Only as he is left truly free to think can he evolve the faith that is right for him. Our task is to surround him with "a particular kind of fellowship" and trust God for the eventual outcome.

THE NATIVITY STORIES

A third-grade class in church school were listing all the stories about Jesus that they knew. Several had mentioned familiar stories. One boy said, "Oh, and the stories about the night he was born—when the angels sang in the sky."

Harry spoke up, suddenly and positively. "But I don't believe in angels and stuff like that," he said.

Sooner or later every child comes to the point where he is trying to sort out facts from fancies; where he is constantly

[1] *A Call to What Is Vital* (New York: The Macmillan Company, 1948), p. 113.

asking, "Is that true?" "Did that really happen?" And when that time comes he needs honest answers. Sometimes the only honest answer is, "We don't know"; sometimes an honest answer involves a long explanation. Very seldom is a simple "Yes" or "No" an adequate answer to a child's search for understanding.

One would hope that every child might be helped to an *understanding* appreciation of the Nativity stories before he feels pushed to declare, a bit belligerently, "But I don't believe in angels and stuff like that!"

These precious birth stories are so much a part of our joyous Christmas season that all children are familiar with them almost from infancy. Parents will be wise to watch for opportunities to explain casually, and more than once, how these stories came to be written, before the child reaches the "Is it true?" stage. It may be that, by incorporating our understandings and interpretations with the use of the stories from the beginning, the child may be saved from an unwholesome shock later.

We can admit freely that no one really knows just what happened the night Jesus was born. These lovely Christmas stories were written many years later. They grew up among his early followers who loved him dearly. They remembered how he had loved everyone. They remembered how brave and fearless he had been. They knew how their own lives had been changed because they had known him. They knew how he had helped many people—how fearful and anxious people had grown joyful; how weak people had grown strong; how evil people had come to live righteously; how people filled with hate had learned to live with love. These friends of Jesus knew that because of him the whole world would ever after be different and better. No wonder it seemed to them that the night he was born must have been strange and wonderful. Surely no other night in all the centuries could have been like it!

Today we may not believe in angels with feathery wings (save as a lovely symbol) or in a star that moves across the sky to one particular stable, but we love these stories because we know that what they are really saying *is* true; that the night Jesus was born was truly the most wonderful night the world has ever known, because in him God's all-powerful, redeeming love broke through into human experience. No wonder worshiping people felt the need of a heavenly proclamation! How truly they embodied in these poetic stories the truth of the Savior's coming to *all* men, to the humble, adoring shepherds, and to the majestic and equally adoring kings from far places!

With some such interpretations a child may be helped to keep his love of these stories into his adult years, to see in them symbols of imperishable truths, and to enter with joyful understanding into the treasures of art and music and literature through which the original stories, like light passing through a prism, have been glorified in countless rainbow-tinted expressions.

THE MIRACLES

A second group of stories with which boys and girls will need help is that of the miracles. What answers you give to your children's questions must of course depend upon your own belief. Only out of your own heart-searchings can you find the wisdom to meet their needs. If you believe all the miracles happened exactly as they are recounted in the Bible, then obviously that is what you will tell your children and you will not recognize any need for explanations or interpretation.

Even the parent who thus believes, however, will be wise to suggest that, in this matter, opinion is divided. "This is what I believe." But the intellectually honest parent will feel impelled to add, "Others think differently."

Many parents will be conscious of uncertainty, never perhaps having thought through their own beliefs. If this is so, surely the wisest plan is to admit your own perplexity. "Did this really happen? I don't know. I've wondered about it often. No one really knows exactly what happened. Perhaps ————." "It seems to me that ————." This approach seems wiser than to take refuge in dogmatic statements, such as, "It's true because the Bible says so."

Time was, and not so long ago, when the miracle stories were told with every vivid detail *in order to prove* that Jesus was "the Son of God." In recent years the shift has been away from this emphasis. The belief in Jesus' divinity or his deity rests not so much on any superhuman powers he may or may not have had as on the unique quality of his relationship to God and to men.

Jesus came to be seen as God-incarnate *not* because he was able to walk on the water, or turn water into wine, or bring back life to the dead. This belief rests more soundly on the recognition that in every act of his life he revealed God's true nature; that his love was a vital, re-creative, redeeming force, overcoming men's indifference, selfishness, unbelief, weakness, and sinfulness, and bringing to men the will and the ability to live changed lives, lives reflecting something of Jesus' own God-awareness and outreaching love; that he held fast to love even when it seemed to have failed him, when he was forsaken, rejected, despised, crucified. It is this divine-human, loving, God-revealing Jesus with whom we want to confront our children.

If emphasis on the entire life of Jesus as a revelation of God himself is kept in mind, the miracle stories present much less difficulty because they are seen to be not crucially important. The healing miracles become chiefly evidence of Jesus' deep concern for suffering people. We need not be afraid to say that we do not understand just *how* he was able to heal. We can turn the attention not to the dramatic element in the healings but to the deep love of which they were the expression.

The exorcisms of "evil spirits" need to be interpreted in the light of our present-day knowledge of mental sickness and its cure. The belief in evil spirits is one from which "the truth has made us free." (John 8:32) The healing of sick minds is completely believable in view of Jesus' own whole-some and sturdy mentality.

The feeding of the multitudes (John 6:4–14) may be told with emphasis on the little boy's gift of his lunch, and again on Jesus' concern for the needs of people. Or it may be thought of as a parable, Jesus himself being the "bread of life." You may wish to add to your own interpretation, "But many people believe ————."

The more difficult stories, the water into wine (John 2:1–12), the walking on the water (Matthew 14:22–27), the calming of the storm (Luke 8:22–25), the cursing of the fig tree (Matthew 21:18–19), may perhaps not be used with children unless they ask about them. A simple statement, "Some of these stories are hard to understand," may be fol-lowed by an explanation, "You know, these stories of Jesus were written years after the events happened. It may be that someone made a mistake or misunderstood."

In considering any of the miracle stories, you may want to comment in some such way as this: "To me Jesus seems unique, not because of any special powers he had, but because in everything he did and said he was able to show God's love for people. He always was sure of what God wanted him to do, and he always did exactly that, no matter what happened to him as a consequence."

Parents are reminded again that for the understanding of particular stories or passages much invaluable help is given in *The Interpreter's Bible.*

The next chapters will deal with three remaining areas of difficulty: the Crucifixion, the Resurrection, and Eternal Life.

CHAPTER 20

The Crucifixion

In attempting to make available to children "the unsearchable riches of Christ" (Ephesians 3:8) for joyous and triumphant living, no parent can afford to evade the innumerable questions children ask about the crucifixion and the related problems of evil and suffering. Answering these questions is a task before which parents do well to stand in reverent awe and deep humility.

"Why did people kill Jesus?" "Why did he have to die?" "Could he have saved himself?" "What do people mean when they say he died *for us?*"

Every honest attempt to answer seems to lead to more questions, each more difficult than the last. No parent will feel qualified to give final answers, but each must answer honestly, sharing whatever depth of understanding he himself has achieved.

Naturally, the answers will vary with the age of the child. We may heartily wish that knowledge of the Crucifixion could be postponed until the child's maturing understanding is somewhat ready to cope with the depths and heights of the mystery involved. It is a futile wish. Children can never be raised in a vacuum. A chance comment by a playmate, a picture in a magazine or in a church bulletin, a crucifix in a store window or in the home of a Roman Catholic friend—

any one of a number of casual happenings may precipitate the questions. The best a parent can do is to prepare himself ahead of time for the inevitable day of questioning.

For many of us today the significance of the Cross is befogged by the clouds of Old Testament ideology which cluster around it. The doctrine of the atonement—that God's wrath at man's sin had to be appeased, and that Jesus was the "sacrificial lamb" through which justice was maintained and God's holiness satisfied—is reflected in many of the hymns and liturgies of the Church. One statement of it is found in the Epistle to the Hebrews:

> But when Christ appeared . . . he entered once for all into the Holy Place, taking not the blood of goats and calves but his own blood, thus securing an eternal redemption. For if the sprinkling of defiled persons with the blood of goats and bulls and with the ashes of a heifer sanctifies for the purification of the flesh, how much more shall the blood of Christ, who through the eternal Spirit offered himself without blemish to God, purify your conscience from dead works to serve the living God. . . . Indeed, under the law almost everything is purified with blood, and without the shedding of blood there is no forgiveness of sins.
>
> (Hebrews 9:11–14, 22)

However meaningful these verses may have been for Jews and Christians in the first century, they fall strangely on our ears today. Some of us instinctively draw back from the idea of Jesus as a "sacrifice" for the sins of mankind, and from the idea of a wrathful God demanding such a sacrifice before a loving relationship with mankind could be re-established. This kind of weighing and measuring guilt and penalties seems to belong more to Yahweh with his "eye for an eye and a tooth for a tooth" justice, than to the loving, forgiving "Father of our Lord, Jesus Christ."

When we seek, however, to find a way of describing in terms acceptable to modern thinking the profound depth and mystery of the Cross, we flounder helplessly. We are accustomed, perhaps, to think of Jesus on the Cross as completely separate and apart from God. We are apt to assign to God in our thought the role of Spectator or even Instigator, standing off to one side after having somehow decreed that it was his will that Jesus should drink this cup to the dregs. Perhaps Jesus' own cry, "My God, my God, why hast thou forsaken me?" (Mark 15:34) may have contributed to this conception of God's aloofness.

We forget, or certainly we do not sufficiently realize, that *God was in Christ.* (2 Corinthians 5:19) For those whose theological belief is trinitarian, this is the moment of the supreme and profound significance of the Incarnation. For this means that it is not only Jesus the Son who is suffering upon the Cross, it is also God the Father. "For God so loved the world that he gave his only begotten Son" (John 3:16) might conceivably be restated, "For God so loved the world that he incarnated himself as the Son."

As for those whose belief is nearer theistic unitarianism, it is still possible to believe that "God was in Christ reconciling the world to himself," suffering with him in all the depths of agony as any human parent would suffer under similar circumstances.

Halford E. Luccock has called attention to a strange and too seldom recognized fact in the following statements:

> Part of the Christian's saving force in the world is a Christlike sensitiveness to human need that brings real pain into life. To expose our nerves to the hurt of others, to load their burdens onto our shoulders already laden, to let the heart be torn with anguish over suffering which we can legally claim is none of our business—that is not easy. But it is the cup from which Jesus drank. Sensitiveness is the mark of development in the biological world. The lonely amoeba does not have it. Neither does the clam. No one ever heard of a clam with a nervous breakdown. There is nothing to break down. With a great price we have obtained this freedom as men—at the price of pain, in a highly developed nervous system. High rank in the Kingdom of God has the same marks, a very highly developed nervous system, the capacity to feel pain in the suffering of others.[1]

[1] From *The Interpreter's Bible*, Vol. 7, p. 814. Copyright 1951 by Pierce and Smith (Abingdon Press).

To recognize this growing "capacity to feel pain in the suffering of others" as a high development in ourselves, and to fail to recognize in God a similar capacity to suffer is to imply that the creature can rise higher than his Creator.

Surely so to see God as at least a co-sufferer with Jesus does away with the persistent and evil image of God sitting on a throne in the sky, demanding or permitting the crucifixion of Jesus as a necessary atonement for the sins of mankind.

SOME HELPS FOR PARENTS

In the remaining part of this chapter an effort will be made in the light of the foregoing considerations to suggest some ideas and points of view which may be helpful to parents in giving answers to children's specific questions. No interpretation of these deep matters can ever be simple—we are dealing with profound mysteries. The truth we reveal to immature minds may necessarily be limited and fragmentary—it can still be *truth* so far as we are able to discern it.

"Why did Jesus have to die?"

We believe that he did not *have* to die. We believe that it was within his power to turn aside and choose an easier path. We believe he went to Jerusalem with open eyes, knowing the probable end of his journey. We believe he deliberately accepted the Cross as the logical outcome of his life, the final perfect testimony of the "good news" he came to proclaim.

> Jesus chose to go to Jerusalem. . . . the sight of that face "set like flinty stone" to go to Jerusalem struck awe and fear. Courage was in it: the high courage of lonely consecration. Obedience was in it: he would do the Father's will and drink the bitter cup. Redemptive love was in it: he would die in utter love for God and man. Between the lines we can read the voluntariness of the act. He could have gone to Galilee instead of to Jerusalem. He could have chosen safety, with long years of settled teaching, instead of death; and that safe choice could have been plausibly justified. He stood at the fork of the road, and

chose the dangerous right instead of the plausible wrong. He cast the vote of his life for an abandon to God's will, instead of following man's apparently wise "wisdom". . . . "The good shepherd giveth his life for the sheep. . . . No man taketh it from me, but I lay it down of myself." (John 10:11, 18)[2]

"Why then did Jesus choose to die?"

To say in answer to this question, "Because he believed it to be God's will," is too easy even though true. Certainly his prayer in Gethsemane is a clear indication that he did so believe. "Father, if thou art willing, remove this cup from me; nevertheless not my will, but thine, be done." (Luke 22:42) But this answer only leads to another "Why?" "Why was it God's will?"

Apparently Jesus saw his life task to be the revelation of God in human form. "He who has seen me has seen the Father." (John 14:9) He was to show men, "This is God. *God is love*"—love raised to and far beyond the best and highest human love ever known; love reaching out, not just to those who respond, but love active, steadfast, unfailing, even when exposed to the worst and cruelest evil the wicked hearts of men can devise.

That kind of divine love cannot be revealed except in extremity. It can be talked about, admired, accepted theoretically as desirable; but it cannot be *revealed* except in the actual struggle of human living. It has been *perfectly* revealed only in the unique, sublime, voluntary acceptance of the rejection, desertion, humiliation, and physical and spiritual agony of the Cross.

Jesus accepted the Cross because he loved people. He loved the weak and the strong, the cowardly and the brave, the foolish and the wise, the ignorant and the learned, the stupid and the understanding. He loved them so much that to bring them the "good news"—the truth of God's love for them—no price was too high to pay. He accepted the Cross

[2] George A. Buttrick, "Commentary on the Gospel According to Matthew." From *The Interpreter's Bible,* Vol. 7, p. 493. Copyright 1951 by Pierce and Smith (Abingdon Press).

because only by this sublime acceptance could he reveal in all its wholeness the suffering love of God, confronted by the malignant powers of evil, and remaining immovable, unchanged, triumphant.

"What do people mean when they say Jesus died 'for us'?"

No parent can answer this easily or glibly. Books have been written struggling with this question and again parents must answer according to their deepest convictions.

A partial answer might be something like this: "Jesus wanted to show everyone, all people everywhere, and all people who would be born later on through all the ages, that God's love is the most powerful force in all the world, that no evil, or cruelty, or hatred could possibly change it. So you and I today can remember Jesus' prayer, 'Father, forgive them, for they know not what they do,' and we can say, 'That's what God's love is like. And to be God's children that's the kind of love we must try to have.'"

"But why did people want to kill Jesus?"

If it is true that Jesus' whole purpose was to reveal the divine love of God for people, how could it be that people wanted to kill him?

Just because Jesus loved so deeply, he stood unalterably opposed to everything that hurt or oppressed the "little people" of his world. To see the good life—the life lived in loving obedience to the Heavenly Father—reduced to the observance of hundreds of petty rules, was intolerable to him. To see injustice, greed, dishonesty, cruelty in high places drew forth his condemnation. His way of living cut across social procedures; he fraternized with social outcasts; he openly criticized the religious leaders of his day.

His was no sentimental "sweetness and light" ministry. Jesus' teachings and actions were revolutionary. He upset established conditions; he overthrew cherished conventions; he struck at accepted practices and procedures. "The common people heard him gladly," (Mark 12:37, KJ) but the rulers, the established, powerful leaders in political and religious circles, rightly saw in this impassioned Galilean a threat to their privileged positions, a menace which they dared not ignore.

These are partial answers, but the whole problem of evil cannot be so easily handled.

The Bible is full of stories of people who deliberately chose to do evil—Adam and Eve eating the forbidden fruit, Jacob cheating Esau, the brothers of Joseph selling him into slavery, the Israelites worshiping the Golden Calf, David contriving the death of Uriah, Judas betraying Jesus. The list is endless.

Why did all these people choose evil instead of good? We do not know. Only as we search for meaning in life we dimly perceive that *freedom to choose* is perhaps the most startling of man's God-given capacities. God could have made us mere puppets, incapable of either good or evil. But if we were to be capable of creative good it was necessary that we should be free to choose evil. Dimly we perceive the need for testing. Virtue untried is no virtue. Courage that has never been put to the test is not courage. Faith that has never been shaken by doubt is no faith. And the will to choose God as our highest value grows strong only as it struggles against unworthy choices, fails, repents, struggles again.

The problem of evil in its last analysis is personal, and its explanation and meaning must be sought in ourselves. "Why did people want to kill Jesus?" We do not know. Only we recognize in ourselves the disheartening failure to choose the best, the frightening strength of evil impulses, the potential capacity for evil-doing, the desperate need for forgiveness and for renewal of our will for good.

CHAPTER 21

The Resurrection

Now I would remind you, brethren, in what terms I preached to you the gospel. . . . For I delivered to you as of first importance what I also received, that Christ died for our sins in accordance with the scriptures, that he was buried, that he was raised on the third day in accordance with the scriptures, and that he appeared to Cephas [another name for Peter] then to the twelve. Then he appeared to more than five hundred brethren at one time, most of whom are still alive, though some have fallen asleep. Then he appeared to James, then to all the apostles. Last of all, as to one untimely born, he appeared also to me. For I am the least of the apostles, unfit to be called an apostle, because I persecuted the church of God. But by the grace of God I am what I am, and his grace toward me was not in vain. (1 Corinthians 15:1, 3–10)

So writes Paul to the Church in Corinth, probably less than twenty-five years after Jesus was crucified.

This is the earliest written mention of the resurrection that has come down to us. It is interesting to note that in this earliest record no reference is made to an empty tomb, to a physical body, to the eating of food. Here we have only a quiet statement, almost matter-of-fact, it seems, of this soul-shaking event.[1]

Turning from this earliest mention of the resurrection ap-

[1] Paul's own meeting with the risen Christ is described twice, the first time in Acts 9 and the second time in Acts 26, where the story is given in Paul's own words as part of his defense before Agrippa.

pearances to the stories in the Gospels (written a number of years later) we find a growing confusion in the accounts.

In Mark, the earliest of the Gospels to be written, three women go to the tomb and see "a young man." (16:1, 5) In the last verses of Mark (usually agreed to be a later editorial addition) Jesus appears "first to Mary Magdalene." (16:9) "After this he appeared in another form" to two of the disciples. (16:12) Again he appeared to the eleven. (16:14)

In Matthew, "Mary Magdalene and the other Mary" go to the sepulchre (28:1), and talk with "an angel of the Lord." (28:2–7) And as they go to tell the disciples, Jesus meets them. (28:9) Then the eleven disciples go to Galilee and when Jesus appears to them they worship him. (28:17)

In Luke "the women who had come with him from Galilee" (23:55) go to the tomb (24:1) and find "two men in dazzling apparel" (24:4) who give them the news. In Luke also, and only in Luke, is the lovely story of the two disciples on the road to Emmaus (24:13–53) where mention is made of "some women" who had gone early to the tomb and seen "a vision of angels." (24:22–23) Later, apparently the same day, according to Luke, Jesus appears "to the eleven and those who were with them" in Jerusalem (24:36) and eats with them. (24:41–43)

In John, the last of the Gospels to be written, Mary Magdalene goes alone to the tomb (20:1), finds it empty, goes and tells Peter and "the other disciple, the one whom Jesus loved" who run to the tomb with her, find it empty, and then return to their homes. Mary, standing weeping outside the tomb, looks in and sees "two angels in white" (20:12); and later recognizes Jesus himself in the supposed gardener. (20:15–18) John next records Jesus' appearance "on the evening of that same day" (20:19) to the disciples, "the doors being shut" (20:19); a second appearance "eight days later" when Thomas was present (20:26); and another appearance by the Sea of Tiberias where the risen Christ shares a meal of fried fish. (21:1–14)

BEGIN WITH THE POSITIVE TRUTH

It is quite obvious from this brief sketch of the Gospel stories that there is no one direct, easily authenticated account of what happened on Easter morning and in the days immediately following. Details are confusing and contradictory. Because of this difficulty, the parent may feel it wise to begin with children with an emphasis on the positive and undeniable truth in some such terms as these:

"No one knows exactly what happened, but the disciples had some experience that convinced them that Jesus was still alive. They were so sure of it that they were no longer frightened and sick at heart. They were excited and joyous, and suddenly so courageous that they went right back into the very courtyards of the temple and began to proclaim to everyone who would listen the joyous good news!"[2]

John Oxenham has given us the true picture:

> His followers had fled like frightened sheep,
> Their hopes all wrecked by the catastrophe;
> And yet, within a little span of days,
> They were all bound together and to him
> In fellowship far closer than before;
> And, bold beyond their natures, and aflame
> With new-born zeal that burned like pure white fire,
> They faced the world prepared to live and die
> To bring to man the Kingdom of God's Love.
> They were new men, remade, and wholly filled
> With that great spirit that had been their Chief's.
>
> They had sore doubted; they had feared and fled;
> Their hearts had turned to water when he died;
> They had lost hope; and faith, too hardly tried,
> Had sped and left them bruised and stupefied;—
> But now . . . they knew!—they knew!—
> They had been weak,—but now they were like gods,

[2] See the author's *Good News to Tell*, an attempt to embody this point of view in story form for children. (Philadelphia: The Westminster Press, 1949.)

Performing wonders in the name of God,
And preaching everywhere their risen Lord
In words that pierced like lightning to men's hearts.
And all with such vast plenitude of power
That all men marvelled.[3]

In thus emphasizing the *effect* of the resurrection on the disciples we are on firm ground. The proof of the risen Christ does not lie in an empty tomb but in the transformation of the disciples, in the irresistible upsurge of the new faith, in the history of the Church.

As the children come in contact with the resurrection stories, honesty would seem to indicate that the variations in the accounts should be frankly faced. A simple explanation of how the stories have come down to us may be helpful, pointing out the earliest mention in Paul's letter quoted at the beginning of this chapter. We can say, "No one can tell now what really happened. All we can be sure of is that *something did!* All the different stories, and all history since then, testify to one thing: the effect of the risen Christ, first on the disciples, then on the people of the ancient world, and on down through the ages into our own time."

In some such way, perhaps we may be able to preserve "the exclamation point" while dealing honestly with the "question marks."

[3] From *"Gentlemen—The King!"* by John Oxenham. The Pilgrim Press. Used by permission.

CHAPTER 22

Eternal Life

"If a man die, shall he live again?" Job's question has been asked by countless thousands through the centuries, sometimes in obvious disbelief, sometimes in wistful seeking, sometimes in hopeful probing into the mystery of death—and the equal mystery of life.

In *A Guide to Understanding the Bible,* Dr. Fosdick has a chapter on "The Idea of Immortality" which any parent seeking answers to his own, or his children's questions in this area, will find stimulating and helpful. In it he describes at length the Old Testament ideas about life after death and contrasts them with the New Testament faith in eternal life. He says:

> Human beings after death were to the early Hebrews still bodies, attenuated leftovers and shadowy replicas of the flesh.[1]

The Hebrews believed the abode of the dead to be Sheol, definitely located geographically below the earth.

An Old Testament tale tells of the horrible punishment meted out to Korah, Dathan, and Abiram, who had displeased the Lord:

> The ground under them split asunder; and the earth opened its mouth and swallowed them up, with their households and all

[1] P. 257. Used by permission of Harper & Row, Publishers, Incorporated.

the men that belonged to Korah and all their goods. So they and all that belonged to them went down alive into Sheol; and the earth closed over them, and they perished from the midst of the assembly. (Numbers 16:31–33)

Existence in Sheol is almost invariably described in gloomy, hopeless terms. The writer of Ecclesiastes reflects the usual belief when he cautions:

Whatever your hand finds to do, do it with your might; for there is no work or thought or knowledge or wisdom in Sheol, to which you are going." (Ecclesiastes 9:10)

At first Yahweh was thought to have no dominion over Sheol—reason enough for the evident hopelessness.

O Lord, my God, I call for help by day;
 I cry out in the night before thee. . . .
For my soul is full of troubles,
 and my life draws near to Sheol.
I am reckoned among those who go down to the Pit;
 I am a man who has no strength,
like one forsaken among the dead,
 like the slain that lie in the grave,
like those whom thou dost remember no more,
 for they are cut off from thy hand.
Thou hast put me in the depths of the Pit,
 in the regions dark and deep.

PSALMS 88:1, 3–6

One of the few exceptions to this point of view in the Old Testament is in Psalm 139, where the Psalmist cries in a burst of new vision:

Whither shall I go from thy Spirit?
 Or whither shall I flee from thy presence?
If I ascend to heaven, thou art there!
 If I make my bed in Sheol, thou art there!

PSALMS 139:7–8

Occasional flickers of this kind only tend to throw into deeper shadow the usual Old Testament beliefs about Sheol. More typically, Isaiah taunts the king of Babylon:

How the oppressor has ceased,
   the insolent fury ceased!

         . . .

Sheol beneath is stirred up
   to meet you when you come,
it rouses the shades to greet you,
   all who were leaders of the earth;
it raises from their thrones
   all who were kings of the nations.
All of them will speak
   and say to you:
"You too have become as weak as we!
   You have become like us!"
Your pomp is brought down to Sheol,
   the sound of your harps;
maggots are the bed beneath you,
   and worms are your covering.
                ISAIAH 14:4, 9–11

Turning to the New Testament we find a new, contrasting belief in eternal life. Jesus taught that each person was "of value" (Matthew 10:31; Luke 12:7) to God—that God was like a loving Father, actively reaching out to each individual.[2] He said (and this is reported in all three of the synoptic Gospels) that God is the God of Abraham, and Isaac, and Jacob, and added, "He is not God of the dead but of the living." (Matthew 22:32, Mark 12:27, Luke 20:38)

The New Testament belief in eternal life grew surely and strongly out of these teachings of Jesus and out of the God-relatedness of his own life, which his followers caught by contagion. Once faith had convinced them that God enters into loving, personal relationship with each of his creatures, belief in the permanence of that relationship followed almost inevitably.

The New Testament declares that eternal life is the free gift of God through Jesus Christ.

[2] See the parables of the forgiving father (Luke 15:11–32), the lost coin (Luke 15:8–10), the lost sheep (Luke 15:3–7).

> For God so loved the world that he gave his only Son, that whoever believes in him should not perish but have eternal life. (John 3:16)
>
> And this is the testimony, that God gave us eternal life, and this life is in his Son. He who has the Son has life; he who has not the Son has not life. I write this to you who believe in the name of the Son of God, that you may know that you have eternal life. (1 John 5:11–13)

The New Testament declares that eternal life is here and now—that it has already begun.

Jesus said:

> I assure you that the man who trusts in him [the Father] has eternal life already. (John 6:47)[3]

And Again:

> Truly, truly, I say to you, he who hears my word and believes him who sent me, has eternal life; he . . . has passed from death to life. (John 5:24)

Paul writes:

> If any one is in Christ, he is a new creation; the old has passed away, behold, the new has come. (2 Corinthians 5:17)

This new life in Christ is a life lived in the knowledge of God. In his prayer for his disciples, just before his death, Jesus said:

> And this is eternal life, that they know thee the only true God, and Jesus Christ whom thou hast sent. (John 17:3)

This eternal life is characterized by "patience in well-doing." Paul writes:

> For he will render to every man according to his works: to those who by patience in well-doing seek for glory and honor and immortality, he will give eternal life. (Romans 2:6–7)

It is a life set free from bondage to sin. Paul says:

> Yet, though sin is shown to be wide and deep, thank God his grace is wider and deeper still! The whole outlook changes—sin

[3] From *The New Testament in Modern English*, Copyright J. B. Phillips, 1958. Used by permission of The Macmillan Company.

used to be the master of men and in the end handed them over to death: now grace is the ruling factor, with righteousness as its purpose and its end the bringing of men to the eternal life of God through Jesus Christ. (Romans 5:20–21, Phillips)

Eternal life is a life of obedience to God.

He who does the will of God abides for ever. (1 John 2:17)

Eternal life, now and always, is full of joy. Jesus said:

I came that men may have life and may have it in all its fullness. (John 10:10, N.E.)

And again:

These things I have spoken to you, that my joy may be in you, and that your joy may be full. (John 15:11)

Paul testifies:

Through him [Jesus] we have confidently entered into the new relationship of grace, and here we take our stand, in happy certainty of the glorious things he has for us in the future. This doesn't mean, of course, that we have only a hope of future joys—we can be full of joy here and now even in our trials and troubles. Taken in the right spirit these very things will give us patient endurance; this in turn will develop a mature character, and a character of this sort produces a steady hope, a hope that will never disappoint us. Already we have some experience of the love of God flooding through our hearts by the Holy Spirit given to us. (Romans 5:2–5, Phillips)

Be happy in your faith at all times. (1 Thessalonians 5:16, Phillips)

The eternal life is a life of love:

We know that we have passed out of death into life, because we love the brethren. He who does not love remains in death. (1 John 3:14)

Jesus said:

As the Father has loved me, so have I loved you; abide in my love. (John 15:9)

This is my commandment, that you love one another as I have loved you. (John 15:12)

This then is the Christian's hope for eternal life—a quality of life in relationship to God, partially attainable here and now and continuing beyond the incident of physical death—a life marked by growing faith in God and in Jesus Christ, free from the bondage of sin, characterized by patience in well-doing, by obedience to God's will, by love and by deep joy. Eternal life is the free gift of God, part of the "unsearchable riches of Christ" (Ephesians 3:8) which parents may appropriate for themselves and share with their children.

This faith in eternal life still leaves many questions unanswered. What about people who refuse the offered gift of eternal life? What about evil-doers who because of heredity and the failures of society have never had a chance to know love? What about those who have lived in total ignorance of Jesus and the God he reveals? To these and many other questions no fully satisfactory answers may be found.

IDEAS OF HEAVEN AND HELL

Because children sooner or later are bound to come in contact with ideas of "heaven" and "hell," some consideration of these ideas may be helpful.

In the beginning, the idea of life after death seems to have carried with it no thought either of punishment or reward. These beliefs seem to have grown out of the conviction of God's righteousness and justice, as a necessity to balance up the obvious inequities of the present life.

In the parable of the Last Judgment, Matthew 25:31–46, Jesus made use of current Jewish thinking in picturing rewards and punishments in the afterlife. It may be noted, however, that Jesus used this imagery not primarily to give a blueprint of life after death, but rather to describe vividly and unforgettably the qualities of the good life here on earth.

The idea of eternal punishment suggested by the parable must surely be seen as completely contradictory to God's whole nature as revealed in Jesus.

"Depart from me . . . into the eternal fire! . . . and they will go away into eternal punishment." (41, 46)

In commenting on these verses in *The Interpreter's Bible,* Dr. George A. Buttrick points out that the Greek words "do not necessarily imply a finality." They

> may have the meaning of remedial, although severe pruning rather than of arbitrary and vindictive torment (the God and Father of Jesus is neither arbitrary nor vindictive) . . . But the shadows, however we try to soften them, are still deep. We must not make a theology from details of a parable, but by the same token we must be honest with the darkness of the punishment. *Depart* is a terrible word; *come* has all heaven's light and love.[4]

Consequences of evil-doing there must be, of course. Redemptive suffering for sin is a fact easily recognized even in this present life, but hopeless, everlasting torment is surely a hideous misrepresentation of God's way of working with his creatures. It was a wise person indeed who achieved the deep insight that "the existence of hell surely makes heaven impossible."[5]

Even the complete extinction of evil-doers sometimes suggested in place of eternal punishment seems a questionable procedure. Once having bestowed the gift of eternal life, would a loving Father-God withdraw it? No human parent could face such an ultimate outcome for a child, no matter how willful or disobedient. Is it too much to expect greater-than-human love from God? May we not at least cherish the hope that given eternity in which to work an all-wise, loving God will devise ways of winning back to sonship even the worst and most depraved prodigals?

In this whole area of the survival of individuality after death, we are faced with deep mysteries and unanswerable questions. To believe in eternal life is not necessarily to be-

[4] From *The Interpreter's Bible,* Vol. 7, p. 564. Copyright 1951 by Pierce and Smith (Abingdon Press).
[5] Herbert H. Farmer in *God and Men* (Nashville: Abingdon-Cokesbury Press, 1947), p. 169.

lieve in any specific picture of what life after death may be like.

David MacLennan reminds us

> that in all we say concerning the life-beyond-life we must observe the wise reticence of our Lord and of the New Testament. No road-maps of the New Jerusalem have been furnished. On the authority of Christ we can "project a curve" and on the basis of God's mercy of which we have had large experience here, indicate characteristics of the heavenly kingdom we have a right to expect. Employment of our powers rather than celestial stagnation is promised: "They serve Him day and night in His temple." (Revelation 7:15) There will be development, a chance to complete life's unfinished symphony; does He not aim to bring us to perfection, to "the measure of development which belongs to the fullness of Christ"? (Ephesians 4:13, Goodspeed translation) In that perfect relationship we shall have joy unshadowed; did the Master not bid the righteous "enter into the joy of thy Lord"? (St. Matthew 25:21) And the Compassionate Father Himself "shall wipe away all tears from their eyes." (Revelation 11:4)[6]

[6] David A. MacLennan, in *A Preacher's Primer.* (New York: Oxford University Press, 1950), p. 62.

CONCLUSION

The first part of this book dealt with the establishment and maintenance of a Christian family fellowship. The second part was concerned with the parents' task in making the Bible "come alive" for the children.

These two parts are closely related. Concentration on the Bible is not an end in itself but is a means to an end, namely, that the spiritual resources in the Bible may be drawn upon by each member of the family and by the family as a whole to make the family life increasingly a truly redemptive fellowship.

This is a living Gospel with which we are dealing—a living Gospel for the guidance of living persons. As parents themselves succeed in assimilating the Gospel as the source and sustenance of their daily lives, the children may also find in it the essential food for sturdy, wholesome growth.

No task in life can possibly afford such a depth of satisfaction as that of bringing up children "in the discipline and instruction of the Lord." (Ephesians 6:4) For this is a task which shares in the creativity of God himself. With all its anxieties and heartaches, its struggles and failures, it yet affords unique opportunity for achieving the deep and abiding joy repeatedly promised to those who lay hold on the truths of the Gospel:

> These things I have spoken to you, that my joy may be in you, and that your joy may be full. (John 15:11)

APPENDIX I

Approximate Chronology of the Bible Writings

In studying the Bible it is interesting to realize that the writings spread over more than 1000 years.[1]

Before the time of David, 1000 B.C.
A number of brief passages, songs, lyrics, oracles, and sayings; possibly some records of ancestral traditions: notations of legal customs.

Between 1000 B.C. and 700 B.C.
Stories of Saul, David, and Solomon, parts of 1 and 2 Samuel and of 1 Kings.
Some songs and parables, such as the song of praise for David's victories (1 Samuel 18:7); Nathan's parable (2 Samuel 12:1–4); David's lamentation over the death of Saul and Jonathan (2 Samuel 1:19 ff.).
Some laws: the Decalogue of Exodus 34.
The Judean Document of early narratives (Yahwist) about 850 B.C., and the Ephraimitic Document (Eloist) about 750 B.C.
Writings of the prophets—Amos, Hosea, Isaiah of Jerusalem, and Micah.

From 700 B.C. to the fall of Jerusalem, 597 B.C.
Editorial combinations and completions—combination of the Judean and Ephraimitic narratives; first edition of the Book of Kings.
Laws—Deuteronomy.
Writings of the prophets—Zephaniah, Jeremiah, Nahum, Habakkuk.

From 597 B.C. to the rebuilding of the walls of Jerusalem, 444 B.C.
Editorial work, combination of materials with first six books of the Bible. Stories of Joshua, Judges, Samuel.
Laws—"Holiness Code" and Priestly Code.
Writings of the prophets—Jeremiah, Ezekiel, Isaiah of Babylon (40–55), Haggai, Zechariah (1–8), Malachi, Obadiah, Isaiah (55–66).

[1]A more detailed chronology (on which this one is based) will be found in *A Guide to Understanding the Bible*, pages 301–3.

From 444 B.C. *to 100* B.C.

History—memoirs of Nehemiah and Ezra.

Poetry and general literature—Ruth, Proverbs, Job, Esther, Song of Solomon, Jonah, Ecclesiastes, completed Book of Psalms.

Writings of the prophets—Joel, Zechariah.

OF THE NEW TESTAMENT WRITINGS

Before the Gospels

Early collection of the sayings of Jesus, and notes on his life, possibly in Aramaic.

Epistles of Paul, A.D. 50–60, 1 and 2 Thessalonians, Galatians, Corinthian correspondence (probably four letters now combined in two), Romans, Colossians, Philemon, Ephesians, Philippians.

From A.D. *70 to* A.D. *150*

The Gospel According to Mark, about A.D. 70.

The Epistle to the Hebrews, about A.D. 80–90.

The Gospel According to Matthew, A.D. 90–95.

The Gospel According to Luke, and The Acts, about A.D. 90.

The Book of Revelation, about A.D. 95.

1 Epistle of Peter, about A.D. 96.

Epistle of James, about A.D. 100.

The Gospel According to John and the three Epistles of John, about A.D. 100.

The Epistle of Titus, and the two Epistles of Timothy, about A.D. 100, with earlier genuine portions from Paul probably included.

The Epistle of Jude, uncertain.

The 2 Epistle of Peter, about A.D. 150.

APPENDIX II

A Partial Concordance of Bible Material

For any thorough study of the Bible, access to a concordance and a commentary is necessary. This listing of some of the Bible material may prove useful, however, when children need help in finding stories or passages and no concordance is immediately available:

NEW TESTAMENT

God, idea of, in New Testament
Father, loving, forgiving (Prodigal
Son)   Luke 15:11–32

Impartial (sun and rain)	Matthew 5:45
Actively seeking (lost sheep)	Matthew 18:12–14
	Luke 15:4–7
Giver of good gifts	Matthew 7:7–11
"Who shall separate us?"	Romans 8:35–39
Spirit	John 4:24
Incarnate in Christ	John 1:1–5, 14; 14:6–11
Love	1 John 4:16, 18
"In whom we live"	Acts 17:28
Caring for every "little one"	Matthew 18:14
Universal	Revelation 5:9–10
one flock, one shepherd	John 10:16
east, west, north, south	Luke 13:29

Jesus

Nativity stories

Annunciation	Matthew 1:18–21
	Luke 1:26–38
Mary's Magnificat	Luke 1:46–55
Journey to Bethlehem	Luke 2:1–5
Birth	Luke 2:6–7
Shepherds	Luke 2:8–20
Presentation in temple	Luke 2:22–40
Wise men	Matthew 2:1–12
Flight into Egypt	Matthew 2:13–15
Return to Nazareth	Matthew 2:19–23
Trip to Jerusalem	Luke 2:41–52
Baptism	Matthew 3:13–17
	Mark 1:9–11
	Luke 3:21–22
	John 1:29–34
Temptation	Matthew 4:1–11
	Mark 1:12–13
	Luke 4:1–13

Ministry

Calling of disciples	Matthew 4:18–22; 9:9; 10:1–4
	Mark 1:16–20; 2:13–14; 3:13–19
	John 1:40–47
Day in Capernaum	Mark 1:21–34
Blessing the children	Matthew 19:13–15
	Mark 10:13–16
	Luke 18:15–17
"He has anointed me"	Luke 4:18–19
Rejection at Nazareth	Matthew 13:53–58
	Mark 6:1–6
	Luke 4:16–30
At prayer	Matthew 14:23
	Mark 1:35–38
Gethsemane	Mark 14:36, 38
Last Supper	John 17
From the Cross	Luke 23:34, 46
Teaching from a boat	Luke 5:1–3
Teaching on the mountain	Matthew 5, 6, 7

Zacchaeus	Luke 19:1–10
Miracles	
Exorcisms	Matthew 8:28–34; 9:32–34
Feeding multitude	Matthew 15:32–38
	Mark 8:1–9
	Luke 9:12–17
	John 6:5–14
Healing	
Centurion's servant	Matthew 8:5–13
	Luke 7:1–10
Paralytic	Matthew 9:2–8
	Mark 2:1–12
	Luke 5:17–26
Peter's wife's mother	Matthew 8:14–16
	Mark 1:29–34
	Luke 4:38–39
Ten lepers	Luke 17:11–19
Blind	Matthew 9:27–30
	Mark 8:22–26
	Luke 7:21–22
	John 9
Stilling storm	Matthew 8:23–27
	Mark 4:35–41
	Luke 8:22–25
Walking on water	Matthew 14:22–27
	Mark 6:45–51
Water into wine	John 2:1–12
Palm Sunday	Matthew 21:1–11
	Mark 11:1–10
	Luke 19:28–40
	John 12:12–19
Cleansing the Temple	Matthew 21:12–13
	Mark 11:15–17
	Luke 19:45
	John 2:13–17
Widow's mite	Mark 12:41–44
	Luke 21:1–4
Washing disciples' feet	John 13:2–17
Last Supper	Matthew 26:17–30
	Mark 14:17–31
	Luke 22:1–38
	John 13–17
Gethsemane	Matthew 26:36–56
	Mark 14:32–42
	Luke 22:39–53
	John 18:1–13
Peter's denial	Matthew 26:69–75
	Mark 14:66–72
	Luke 22:54–62
	John 18:15–18, 25–27

Trial before Annas and Caiaphas	Matthew 26:57–68
	Mark 14:53–65
	Luke 22:66–71
	John 18:12–14, 19–24
Trial before Pilate	Matthew 27:1–2, 11–26
	Mark 15:1–15
	Luke 23:1–25
	John 18:28–40; 19:1–16
Crucifixion	Matthew 27:27–56
	Mark 15:16–41
	Luke 23:26–49
	John 19:17–37
Resurrection	Matthew 28
	Mark 16
	Luke 24
	John 20, 21
	1 Corinthians 15:1–10
	Galatians 1:11–17
Teachings	
Beatitudes	Matthew 5:1–11
	Luke 6:20–23
Commandments, Two	Matthew 22:34–40
	Mark 12:28–34
	Luke 10:25–28
Cup of cold water	Matthew 10:42
	Mark 9:41
Golden Rule	Matthew 7:12
	Luke 6:31
Good Samaritan	Luke 10:25–37
"I am the way"	John 14:6
"Inasmuch . . ."	Matthew 25:40
Judgment, last	Matthew 25:31–46
Kingdom teachings	Matthew 13:24–52
	Mark 4:26–32
	Luke 17:20–21
Lord's Prayer	Matthew 6:5–15
	Luke 11:1–4
"Love one another"	John 13:34–35; 15:12–14
"Not to be ministered unto"	Matthew 20:28 (KJ)
	Mark 10:45
Prodigal Son	Luke 15:11–32
Reminders of the faith	
Birds of the air	Matthew 6:26
Bread of life	John 6:35
Bread and wine	Matthew 26:26–28
House on rock	Matthew 7:24–27
Leaven	Matthew 13:33
Light, you are the	Matthew 5:14
Lilies of the field	Matthew 6:28
Mustard seed	Matthew 13:31
Salt, you are the	Matthew 5:13
Sheep, lost	Matthew 18:12–14
	Luke 15:4–7

Amalekites	1 Samuel 15:1–4
Amos	Amos 7:14
Ark, Noah's	Genesis 6; 7; 8
Ark of the Covenant	Exodus 37:1–9
Babel, Tower of	Genesis 11:1–9
Cain and Abel	Genesis 4:1–16
Creation	Genesis 1:1–31; 2:1–3
Daniel, stories of	
Handwriting on wall	Daniel 5:1–30
Lion's den	Daniel 6:16–23
David, stories of	
Shepherd boy	1 Samuel 17:34–36
Anointed	1 Samuel 16:1–13
Musician to Saul	1 Samuel 16:14–23
Friend of Jonathan	1 Samuel 18:1–4
Slayer of Goliath	1 Samuel 17:1–50
Spares Saul's life	1 Samuel 26
Bathsheba	2 Samuel 11; 12
Lament over Saul and Jonathan	2 Samuel 1:17–27
Kindness to Jonathan's son	2 Samuel 9
Elijah, stories of	
Fed by ravens	1 Kings 17:1–6
Taken to heaven (fiery chariot)	2 Kings 2:11
Contest with Baal	1 Kings 18:17–39
Elisha, stories of	
Naaman's maid	2 Kings 5:1–14
Ax-head recovered	2 Kings 6:1–7
Fiery furnace	Daniel 3
Flood	Genesis 6:5–22; 7
God, ideas of	
Primitive (conflicting with Christian)	
Angry (flood)	Genesis 6; 7
Destructive (Sodom and Gomorrah)	Genesis 19:24–28
Jealous	Exodus 20:5
Just, but relentless (eye for eye)	Leviticus 24:13–20
Furious	Leviticus 26:14–33
Relentless (Korah, Dathan, Abiram)	Numbers 16:23–32
Merciless (stubborn son)	Deuteronomy 21:18–21
Ruthless (Amalekites)	1 Samuel 15:1–3
Pitiless	Ezekiel 5:8–13
Bestial	Hosea 13:4–8
Vindictive (she-bears)	2 Kings 2:23–24
Unapproachable	Exodus 20:19
From the Prophets (in harmony with Christian)	
Not "visiting iniquities on children"	Ezekiel 18
Not pleased with empty ritual	Amos 5:4–24
	Isaiah 1:12–17

Demanding justice, righteousness	Amos 5:24
	Micah 6:6–8
	Isaiah 1:17
Demanding service to the needy	Isaiah 58:1, 4–9
Forgiving	Isaiah 55:6–11
Universal	Ruth
	Jonah
	Micah 4:1–4
From the Psalms (in harmony with Christian)	
Revealed in Creation	Psalms 19:1–4
Very present help	Psalms 46:1–3
Pitying, as a father	Psalms 103:8–18
Eternal dwelling place	Psalms 90:1–2
Omnipresent	Psalms 139:7–12
Surrounding his people	Psalms 125:1–2
Goliath, slain by David	1 Samuel 17
Hosea	Hosea 11:1–4
Isaac, stories of	
Birth	Genesis 21:1–8
Rebekah	Genesis 24
Digging wells	Genesis 26:18–22
Isaiah—his call	Isaiah 6:1–8
Jacob, stories of	
Buying birthright	Genesis 25:27–34
Deceiving Isaac	Genesis 27
Dream	Genesis 28
Wrestles with angel	Genesis 32:22–32
Father of twelve tribes	Genesis 49
Joseph, stories of	
Coat of many colors	Genesis 37:1–3
Dreams	Genesis 37:5–11
Sold into slavery	Genesis 37:18–36
In Egypt	Genesis 39; 40; 41
Forgives his brothers	Genesis 45
Joshua, walls of Jericho	Joshua 6
Moses, stories of	
Birth and childhood	Exodus 2:1–10
Slays the Egyptian	Exodus 2:11–14
Flight to desert	Exodus 2:15
Meets Zipporah	Exodus 2:16–21
Burning bush	Exodus 3
Frees the Israelites	Exodus 5–15
Red Sea crossing	Exodus 14:10–31
Covenant at Mount Sinai	Exodus 19; 20
Ten Commandments	Exodus 20:1–17
Water from the rock	Numbers 20:1–13
Naaman's maid	2 Kings 5:1–14
Noah's ark	Genesis 6:5–22; 7
Rainbow	Genesis 9:11–17
Samson and Delilah	Judges 16:4–21

BIBLIOGRAPHIES

I. CHILDREN'S BOOKS WITH RELIGIOUS VALUES

In each of the following categories, the titles are arranged roughly in the order of age-interest, beginning with those of interest to the youngest.

Books which may develop an interest in the Bible and life in Bible times:

Entwistle, Mary and Muriel Chalmers. *When Jesus Was a Boy* and *Isaac of the Tents* (Bible Books for Small People). New York: Thomas Nelson and Sons, 1950.

Anderson, Phoebe. *The First Christmas*. Boston, Philadelphia: United Church Press, 1960.

Walker, Janie. *My Bible Book*. Chicago: Rand, McNally & Company, 1946.

Eberling, Georgia Moore. *When Jesus Was a Little Boy*. Chicago: Children's Press, 1954.

Wolcott, Carolyn Muller. *At Jesus' House*. Nashville: Broadman Press, 1959.

Goddard, Carrie Lou. *Jesus Goes to School*. Nashville: Abingdon Press, 1954.

Tippett, James S. *Jesus Lights the Sabbath Lamp*. Nashville: Abingdon-Cokesbury Press, 1953.

Doane, Pelagie. *The Boy Jesus*. New York: Oxford University Press, 1953.

Clarke, Sara Klein. *The Lord Will Love Thee*. Stories of the early Hebrews, "a people who knew that God loved them." Illustrated by Tasha Tudor. Philadelphia: The Westminster Press, 1959.

Fitch, Florence Mary. *The Child Jesus*. New York: Lothrop, Lee & Shepard, 1955.

Hessemer, Betty. *My Story Book About the Bible*. New York: Friendship Press, 1947.

Kunhardt, Dorothy. *Once There Was a Little Boy*. New York: The Viking Press, 1946.

Jones, Jessie Orton. *Small Rain*. Selected verses from the Bible, illustrated by Elizabeth Orton Jones. New York: The Viking Press, 1949.

Smither, Ethel. *Picture Book of Palestine*. Nashville: Abingdon-Cokesbury Press, 1947.

Tudor, Tasha, illustrator. *And It Was So*. Philadelphia: The Westminster Press, 1958.

Taylor, Florence M. *Good News to Tell*. An imaginative story of Mark and his writing of his Gospel. Philadelphia: The Westminster Press, 1949.

Brown, Margaret Wise. *Little Lost Lamb,* illustrated by Leonard Weisgard. Garden City, N.Y.: Doubleday & Company, Inc., 1945.

Eisenberg, Azriel. *The Great Discovery* (the Dead Sea Scrolls). London & New York: Abelard-Schuman, Limited, 1957.

McGavran, Grace. *Stories of the Book of Books*. New York: The Friendship Press, 1947.

Speare, Elizabeth. *The Bronze Bow*. Boston: Houghton-Mifflin Company, 1961.

*Armstrong, April Oursler. *The Book of God: Adventures from the Old Testament*. New York: Doubleday & Company, Inc., 1957. Illustrated.

*Bowie, Walter Russell. *The Bible Story for Boys and Girls—New Testament*. Nashville: Abingdon-Cokesbury Press, 1951.

*————. *The Bible Story for Boys and Girls—Old Testament*. Nashville: Abingdon-Cokesbury Press, 1952.

DeJong, Meindert. *Bible Days*. Grand Rapids, Michigan: Fideler Company, 1948.

Flight, John W. *The Drama of Ancient Israel*. Boston: Beacon Press, 1949.

Witheridge, Elizabeth P. *Mara of Old Babylon*. Nashville: Abingdon Press, 1955.

Klaber, Florence W. *Joseph, the History of Twelve Brothers*. Boston: Beacon Press, 1941.

Allstrom, Elizabeth. *Songs Along the Way*. Nashville: Abingdon Press, 1961.

Chute, Marchette. *Jesus of Israel*. New York: E. P. Dutton & Company, Inc., 1961.

Terrien, Samuel. *Lands of the Bible*. A Golden Historical Atlas. The fully illustrated story of Palestine, and the Middle East. Excellent resource book. New York: Simon and Schuster, Inc., 1957.

*De Angeli, Marguerite. *The Old Testament*. New York: Doubleday & Company, Inc., 1960.

* These Bible story books follow the Bible closely and so need the same explanations and interpretations as the Bible text itself.

Books which may be helpful in developing the inner spiritual life:

Bannister, Constance. *A Child's Grace.* New York: E. P. Dutton & Company, Inc., 1948.

Tudor, Tasha. *First Graces.* New York: Oxford University Press, 1955.

Clough, William. *Father, We Thank Thee.* Nashville: Abingdon Press, 1949.

Clemens, Margaret. *My Prayer Book.* Chicago: Rand, McNally & Co., 1947.

Van Meter, Harriet. *Hands, Hands, Hands,* "Thank you, God, for hands." Illustrated with photographs. Richmond, Va.: John Knox Press, 1958.

Fitch, Florence Mary. *A Book about God.* New York: Lothrop, Lee & Shepard Company, 1953.

Walpole, Ellen Wales. *A First Book about God.* New York: Franklin Watts, Inc., 1950.

Taylor, Florence M. *Thine Is the Glory,* an interpretation of the Lord's Prayer. Philadelphia: The Westminster Press, 1948.

McCauley, Elfrieda and Leon, eds. *A Book of Family Worship.* New York: Charles Scribner's Sons, 1959.

Brooke, Avery. *Youth Talks with God.* New York: Charles Scribner's Sons, 1959.

Books which may help a child understand Christian values in living:

Zolotow, Charlotte. *The Sky Was Blue.* New York: Harper & Row, 1963.

Watts, Mabel. *Over the Hills to Ballybog.* New York: Aladdin Books, 1954.

Anglund, Joan Marsh. *A Friend Is Someone Who Likes You* (1958), *Look Out the Window* (1959), *Love Is a Special Way of Feeling* (1960), *Christmas Is a Time of Giving* (1961). New York: Harcourt, Brace and Company.

Taylor, Florence M. *Growing Pains.* Philadelphia: The Westminster Press, 1948.

Kelly, Eric P. *In Clean Hay.* Illustrated by the Petershams. New York: The Macmillan Company, 1932, 1953.

Crowell, Grace Noll. *Little Boy Down the Lane* (1952), *The Wood Carver* (1954). Minneapolis: The Augsburg Publishing House.

Doane, Pelagie. *St. Francis.* New York: Henry Z. Walck, Inc., 1960.

Books which may help a child develop an understanding of some of life's problems and of creative ways of meeting them:

Sorensen, Virginia. *Miracles on Maple Hill.* New York: Harcourt, Brace & World, Inc., 1957.

Vance, Marguerite. *Windows for Rosemary*. E. P. Dutton & Company, Inc., 1956.

Wright, Anna Rose. *Land of Silence*. New York: Friendship Press, 1962.

McNeer, May and Lynd Ward. *Armed with Courage*. Nashville: Abingdon Press, 1957.

Little, Jean. *Mine for Keeps*. Boston: Little, Brown and Company, 1962.

Books which may help a child develop appreciation of people of other cultural and racial backgrounds:

Millen, Nina. *Around the World Picture Books: Babies around the World; Children and Their Homes; Children and Their Pets; Children and Their Toys; Children at Worship;* several other titles. New York: Friendship Press.

Keats, Ezra Jack. *The Snowy Day*. New York: The Viking Press, 1962.

Jones, Jessie Orton, ed. *This Is the Way*—Prayers and Precepts from World Religions. New York: The Viking Press, 1951.

Fitch, Florence Mary. *One God—The Ways We Worship Him*. New York: Lothrop, Lee & Shepard Company, Inc., 1944.

Perry, George Sessions. *Families of America—Where They Come From and How They Live*. New York: Whittlesey House, McGraw-Hill Book Company, 1949.

McSwigan, Marie. *All Aboard for Freedom!* New York: The Junior Literary Guild and E. P. Dutton & Co., Inc., 1954.

Books which may encourage a child's sense of wonder and develop appreciation of the world in which we live:

Parker, Bertha Morris. *The Basic Science Education Series,* Grades 1 through 9. Laboratory School, University of Chicago. Evanston, Illinois: Row, Peterson and Company, 1941–1958.

Doane, Pelagie, ed. *Littlest Ones*. New York: Oxford University Press, 1956.

Zolotow, Charlotte. *Over and Over*. New York: Harper & Brothers, 1957.

Blough, Glenn O. *Soon after September*. New York: Whittlesey House, McGraw-Hill Book Co., Inc., 1959.

Gay, Zenya. *The Nicest Time of Year*. New York: The Viking Press, 1960.

Rey, H. A. *The Stars*. Boston: Houghton Mifflin Company, 1952.

Bell, Thelma Harrington. *Snow*. New York: The Viking Press, 1954.

Ames, Gerald, and Rose Wyler. *First Days of the World*. New York: Harper & Brothers, 1958.

Stevens, Bertha. *How Miracles Abound,* book and leaflets. Boston: The Beacon Press, 1941.

Foster, Virgil E. *Close-Up of a Honeybee*. New York: Young Scott Books.

II. CHRISTIAN FAMILY LIVING

If you are a woman:

Hilliard, Marion. *A Woman Doctor Looks at Love and Life.* A warm, human book, irradiated by a deep, underlying Christian faith. Garden City, N.Y.: Doubleday & Company, Inc., 1956.

If you are engaged (or hope to be):

Leonard, Wynona Farquar. *Love That Lasts a Lifetime.* Great Neck, N.Y.: Round Table Press, 1961.

Bowman, Henry A. *A Christian Interpretation of Marriage.* Philadelphia: The Westminster Press, 1959.

Thompson, Taliaferro. *An Adventure in Love.* Richmond, Va.: John Knox Press, 1956.

If you are a "young married":

Mace, David R. *Whom God Hath Joined.* Philadelphia: The Westminster Press, 1958.

Howe, Reuel L. *Herein Is Love.* A study of the Biblical doctrine of love in its bearing on personality, parenthood, teaching and all other human relationships. Valley Forge: The Judson Press, 1961.

Winter, Gibson. *Love and Conflict.* New patterns in family life. Analysis and interpretation of the marriage relationship with a strong Biblical orientation. Garden City, N.Y.: Doubleday & Company, Inc., 1958.

If you are about to have your first baby:

Wheatcroft, Anita *Preface for Parents.* Greenwich, Conn.: The Seabury Press, 1955.

Maynard, Donald M. *Your Home Can Be Christian.* Nashville: Abingdon Press, 1952.

Channels, Vera. *The Layman Builds a Christian Home.* St. Louis, Mo.: The Bethany Press, 1959.

If you are a tired mother of toddlers:

Hilliard, Marion. *Women and Fatigue.* A most helpful and comforting book. Garden City, N.Y.: Doubleday & Company, Inc., 1960.

If you are a proud (but bewildered) father:

Johnson, E. Ashby. *Communion with Young Saints.* Conversations, sometimes light, sometimes serious, between a father and his two sons. Richmond, Va.: John Knox Press, 1959.

If you are a mother of daughters:

Evans, Laura Margaret. *Hand in Hand: Mother, Child, and God.* You may not agree at every point with the theology of this book, but you will be moved by the tenderness, the forgiveness, the understanding, which characterize these mother-daughter relationships. Westwood, N.J.: Fleming H. Revell Company, 1950.

If you are a parent with a problem (and what parent isn't?):

Werner, Hazen G. *Christian Family Living.* Nashville: The Graded Press, 1958.

Wynn, John Charles. *How Christian Parents Face Family Problems.* Philadelphia: The Westminster Press, 1955.

Petersen, Sigurd D. *Retarded Children: God's Children.* Philadelphia: The Westminster Press, 1960.

Jones, Eve. *Raising Your Child in a Fatherless Home.* New York: The Free Press of Glencoe, Inc., 1962.

Egelson, Jim and Janet Frank. *Parents Without Partners. A Guide for Divorced, Widowed, or Separated Parents.* New York: E. P. Dutton & Co., 1961.

If you are (or are about to be) a mother-in-law:

Neisser, Edith. *How to Be a Good Mother-in-law and Grandmother.* New York: Public Affairs Pamphlets, #174, 1951.

If you are in the sixty-plus group:

Maves, Paul B. *The Best Is Yet to Be.* Philadelphia: The Westminster Press, 1951.

III. FAMILY WORSHIP

NOTE: Most denominations provide materials for use in worship in the home, and some of these are helpful. Consult your own denomination for their offerings in this area. Many discriminating parents prefer to develop their own materials and procedures to meet the needs and interests of the members of the family. Listed below are several resource books that may prove useful to these parents.

Perkins, Jeannette E. *Children's Worship in the Church School* and *More Children's Worship in the Church School.* Contain a wealth of resource materials, poems, Biblical selections, songs, stories that can be creatively used to enrich worship in the home. New York: Harper & Brothers, 1939, 1953.

Berrey, Lester V., ed. *A Treasury of Biblical Quotations.* New York: Doubleday & Company, Inc., 1958.

Walker, Edith and Aimee Augus Barber, eds. *Thoughts of God for Girls and Boys.* Selections for family worship from the 1936–46 issues of the devotional book published four times a year by the Connecticut Council of Churches. New York: Harper & Brothers, 1946.

McCauley, Elfrieda and Leon, eds. *A Book of Family Worship,* designed for use by parents with children in the home. An excellent foreword by Walter Russell Bowie. This book was developed with the counsel of an interdenominational committee of outstanding qualifications. Some parents may find that this type of formal service does not meet their needs, but all parents can find here a rich source of materials to be used flexibly and creatively. Reverent and lovely prayers, gathered from the treasury of all ages. New York: Charles Scribner's Sons, 1959.

Luccock, Halford E. and Frances Brentano. *The Questing Spirit, Religion in the Literature of Our Time.* New York: Coward-McCann Inc., 1947.

Coffin, Henry Sloane. *Joy in Believing, An Inspirational Treasury,* edited by Walter Russell Bowie. New York: Charles Scribner's Sons, 1956.

Wagenknecht, Edward, ed. *The Story of Jesus in the World's Literature.* An excellent anthology, now out of print, but sometimes available in libraries and second-hand bookstores. New York: Creative Age Press, Inc., 1946.

————. *Stories of Christ and Christmas.* New York: David McKay Company, 1963.

Bro, Margueritte Harmon. *Every Day a Prayer.* New York: Harper & Brothers, 1943.

Gollancz, Victor and Barbara Greene. *God of a Hundred Names: A Collection of Prayers.* New York: Doubleday and Company, Inc., 1963.

IV. BIBLES AND BOOKS ABOUT THE BIBLE

Modern translations of the Bible

The New Testament: An American Translation by Edgar J. Goodspeed. Chicago: The University of Chicago Press, 1923.

The Old Testament: An American Translation. J. M. Powis Smith, ed. Chicago: The University of Chicago Press, 1941.

The Holy Bible, Revised Standard Version. New York: Thomas Nelson & Sons, 1946, 1952.

The Bible: A New Translation by James Moffatt. New York: Harper & Brothers, 1922–35.

The New Testament in Modern English, translated by J. B. Phillips. New York: The Macmillan Company, 1958.

The New English Bible, New Testament. New York: Oxford University Press, 1961.

Shortened forms of the Bible

Olive Pell Bible, condensed from The King James version. New York: Crown Publishers, 1952.

The Short Bible. J. Edgar Goodspeed and J. M. Powis Smith, eds. Chicago: Chicago University Press, 1933.

The Junior Bible. J. Edgar Goodspeed, ed. New York: The Macmillan Company, 1936.

Commentaries and books about the Bible

Gaster, Theodor. *The Dead Sea Scriptures: In English Translations with Introduction and Notes.* New York: Doubleday & Company, Inc., 1956.

The Interpreter's Bible. The Holy Scriptures in the King James and Revised Standard Versions with General Articles and Introduction, Exegesis, Exposition for Each Book of the Bible. 12 vols. Nashville: Abingdon Press, 1952.

Bowie, Walter Russell. *The Story of the Bible.* Nashville: Abingdon Press, 1934.

Burrows, Millar. *The Dead Sea Scrolls.* New York: The Viking Press, 1955.

Fosdick, Harry Emerson. *A Guide to Understanding the Bible.* How the great ideas of God, man, immortality, right and wrong, suffering, worship, and prayer developed in the Bible. New York: Harper & Brothers, 1948; also Torchlight Books, 1956.

Fuller, Reginald H. and G. Ernest Wright. *The Book of the Acts of God: An Introduction to the Bible* (Christian Faith Series). New York: Doubleday & Company, Inc., 1957.

Albright, William F. *From the Stone Age to Christianity.* New York: Doubleday & Company, Inc., 1957.

Anderson, Bernard W. *Rediscovering the Bible.* New York: Association Press, 1951.

Westermann, Claus. *A Thousand Years and a Day.* Philadelphia: Muhlenberg Press, 1962.

Barclay, William. *The Mind of Jesus, The Mind of St. Paul.* New York: Harper & Brothers, 1958, 1961.

The Bible Today. Historical, Social and Literary Aspects of the Old and New Testaments, described by Christian scholars. New York: Harper & Brothers, in co-operation with *The Times,* London, 1955.

Neil, Stephen. *A Genuinely Human Existence.* Toward a Christian Psychology. Garden City, N.Y.: Doubleday & Company, Inc., 1959.

Thielicke, Helmut. *The Parables of Jesus.* New York: Harper & Brothers, 1959.

Daniel-Rops, Henri. *Daily Life in the Time of Jesus.* New York: Hawthorn Books, Inc., 1962.

V. MINISTRY TO FAMILIES

Books for ministers, directors of Christian education, members of family life committees:

Hulme, William E. *The Pastoral Care of Families.* Its theology and practice. Nashville: Abingdon Press, 1962.

Feucht, Oscar E., ed. *Helping Families in the Church.* St. Louis: Concordia Publishing House, 1957.

Wynn, John Charles. *Pastoral Ministry to Families.* Philadelphia: The Westminster Press, 1957.

Wynn, John Charles, ed. *Sermons on Marriage and Family Life.* Nashville: Abingdon Press, 1956.

Fairchild, Roy W. and J. C. Wynn. *Families in the Church.* A Protestant survey. New York: Association Press, 1961.

Duvall, Evelyn M. and M. Sylvanus, eds. *Sex Ways—in Fact and Faith.* Workbook for the North American Conference on Church and Family. New York: Association Press, 1961.

Genne, Elizabeth and William, eds. *Foundations for Christian Family Policy.* The proceedings of the North American Conference on Church and Family. New York: National Council of Churches, 1962.

Arthur, Julietta K. *You and Yours: How to Help Older People.* Philadelphia: J. B. Lippincott Company, Keystone Books, 1960.

Denton, Wallace. *What's Happening to Our Families?* Philadelphia: The Westminster Press, 1963.

Gray, Robert and David Moberg. *The Church and the Older Person.* Grand Rapids, Michigan: Wm. B. Eerdmans Publishing Company, 1962.

Maves, Paul and J. Lennart Cedarleaf. *Older People in the Church.* Nashville: Abingdon-Cokesbury Press, 1959.